COMPARABLE
WORTH
New Directions for Research

COMPARABLE WORTH

New Directions for Research

Heidi I. Hartmann, Editor

Committee on Women's Employment
and Related Social Issues

Commission on Behavioral and
Social Sciences and Education

National Research Council

NATIONAL ACADEMY PRESS
Washington, D.C. 1985

NATIONAL ACADEMY PRESS   2101 Constitution Ave., NW   Washington, DC 20418

This project was supported by the Ford Foundation.

Library of Congress Cataloging in Publication Data
Main entry under title:

Comparable worth.

"Committee on Women's Employment and Related Social
Issues, Commission on Behavioral and Social Sciences and
Education, National Research Council."
Report of and revised papers from the Seminar on
Comparable Worth Research held at Hilton Head, South
Carolina on Oct. 7–8, 1983.
Bibliography: p.
Includes index.
1. Equal pay for equal work—United States—Research—
Congresses. I. Hartmann, Heidi I. II. National
Research Council (U.S.). Committee on Women's
Employment and Related Social Issues. III. Seminar
on Comparable Worth Research (1983: Hilton Head, S.C.)
HD6061.2.U6C653   1985   331.2'1   85–60053

ISBN 0-309-03534-1

Printed in the United States of America

COMMITTEE ON WOMEN'S EMPLOYMENT
AND RELATED SOCIAL ISSUES

PARTICIPANTS, SEMINAR ON
COMPARABLE WORTH RESEARCH

DONALD J. TREIMAN (Chair), Department of Sociology, University of California, Los Angeles

BARBARA R. BERGMANN, Department of Economics, University of Maryland

ALISON BERNSTEIN, Ford Foundation, New York

WILLIAM T. BIELBY, Department of Sociology, University of California, Santa Barbara

MICHAEL H. BIRNBAUM, Department of Psychology, University of Illinois

PAMELA S. CAIN, Department of Sociology, Hunter College, City University of New York

PHOEBE COTTINGHAM, Rockefeller Foundation, New York

HEIDI I. HARTMANN (Study Director), National Research Council

LAWRENCE M. KAHN, Institute of Labor and Industrial Relations, University of Illinois

ROSE S. KAUFMAN (Seminar Coordinator), National Research Council

MARK R. KILLINGSWORTH, Department of Economics, Rutgers University

ROBERT E. KRAUT, Bell Communications Research, Inc., Morristown, N.J.

JUDITH E. KURTZ, Equal Rights Advocates, San Francisco

LESLIE Z. McARTHUR, Department of Psychology, Brandeis University

KATHERINE McKEE, Ford Foundation, New York

NAOMI R. QUINN, Department of Anthropology, Duke University

HELEN REMICK, Office of Affirmative Action, University of Washington

BARBARA F. RESKIN, Department of Sociology, University of Michigan

PATRICIA A. ROOS (Rapporteur), Department of Sociology, State University of New York, Stony Brook

JAMES E. ROSENBAUM, Department of Sociology, Northwestern University

DONALD P. SCHWAB, Graduate School of Business and Industrial Relations Research Institute, University of Wisconsin

BARBARA SMITH, Southeast Women's Employment Coalition, Milton, W.Va.

RONNIE STEINBERG, Center for Women in Government, State University of New York, Albany

Preface

This volume is the result of a seminar on comparable worth research organized by the National Research Council (NRC) Committee on Women's Employment and Related Social Issues and sponsored by the Ford Foundation. The seminar was designed to develop an agenda for social science research related to comparable worth. It was chaired by Donald J. Treiman, professor of sociology at the University of California, Los Angeles, and attended by researchers, including members of the committee, from a variety of disciplines. To provide background for the participants, the committee asked six social scientists to prepare papers on the comparable worth issue assessing the current state of knowledge about comparable worth and related pay equity issues.

This volume includes the report of the seminar, which consists of an agenda of needed research based on discussions at the seminar, as well as revised versions of the papers. The research agenda reflects the overall purpose of the seminar, which was to assess what is known about comparable worth, what is not known, and what the resulting research implications are for social scientists. The seminar, held in October 1983, extended and amplified the work on comparable worth of a previous NRC committee, the Committee on Occupational Classification and Analysis.

The Committee on Women's Employment and Related Social Issues hoped that one major outcome of the seminar would be the stimulation of research activity in the area of comparable worth among basic researchers not currently working in the area. Toward this end, the committee invited scholars from relevant disciplines who represent differing viewpoints. Both those with a demonstrated knowledge of the field and those whose research has not included comparable worth issues were invited. The disciplines represented include anthropology, economics, history, law, psychology, and sociology. In addition, several participants brought to the discussion experience with the practical issues of implementation.

Although the discussion focused on comparable worth, the seminar participants also discussed pay equity strategies more generally. We hope that this report will be useful to a broad range of people with an interest in comparable worth, including social scientists who hope to investigate comparable worth from their own disciplinary (or interdisciplinary) perspectives and practitioners wishing to explore implementation of comparable worth strategies.

ALICE S. ILCHMAN, *Chair*
Committee on Women's Employment
and Related Social Issues

Acknowledgments

The committee is grateful to the Ford Foundation for its financial support of the seminar and of this report, particularly to Amy Vance and Alison Bernstein, program officers for these projects. Although Amy Vance was unable to attend, her conceptions contributed a great deal to the seminar, and we especially appreciate her continued support throughout the process of developing this volume.

I would also like to thank the committee members whose special efforts contributed to this project: Donald J. Treiman, who chaired the seminar and the steering committee that planned it; and Lawrence M. Kahn, Robert E. Kraut, and Naomi R. Quinn, all of whom served on the steering committee and attended the seminar. I would like to convey our thanks especially to all who participated in the seminar as well as to the authors of the papers; without them, of course, the seminar and the report would not have been possible. Our thanks go also to those who wrote the report of the seminar: Heidi I. Hartmann, Patricia A. Roos, and Donald J. Treiman. All members of the committee as well as the seminar participants commented on the draft report, as did members of the Commission on Behavioral and Social Sciences and Education, and to all of them we are grateful.

As is usually the case with collective projects, there were many actors behind the scenes whose efforts were crucial to the successful completion of this project. I would like to mention the contributions of a few of these people and convey our appreciation to Christine L. McShane, editor of the Commission on Behavioral and Social Sciences and Education, for her careful editing of the report and accompanying papers; Eugenia Grohman, the commission's associate director for reports, for her insight and guidance; Rose S. Kaufman, for her attention to all the finer points of meeting arrangements; Lucile DiGirolamo, for her careful consideration of all the steps necessary to produce a final product; and Suzanne Donovan and Rita Conroy, for their essential help in completing the manuscript.

ALICE S. ILCHMAN

Contents

I
Report of a Seminar

An Agenda for Basic Research on Comparable Worth

Heidi I. Hartmann, Patricia A. Roos, and Donald J. Treiman

INTRODUCTION

Background

Beginning in the late 1970s, the question of whether the differences in average wages between jobs held mainly by women and jobs held mainly by men are equitable has come to the fore as a major social issue. Indeed, it was identified as "the civil rights issue of the eighties" by Eleanor Holmes Norton when she was chair of the Equal Employment Opportunity Commission (Norton, 1979). Increasingly the claim is heard that jobs ought to be paid according to their intrinsic worth, as measured by such factors as skill required, responsibility entailed, and effort involved, and that the wage levels of jobs of "comparable worth," that is, equal worth or equal value, ought to be equal.[1]

Concern with the average wage levels of occupations and jobs stems from two relatively unchanging aspects of the labor market: extreme job segregation by sex and the well-known gap in pay between men and women. Considering only workers employed full time year round, women on average earn about 60 percent of what men earn, and this gap shows little sign of

---

[1] Although the issue of comparability can apply to wage differentials between all jobs (e.g., football players and plumbers), this discussion is concerned only with those occupational differentials that are thought to be affected by stereotyping, bias, or discrimination based on sex, race, or ethnicity, and the primary focus is on sex.

3

lessening. Moreover, the sex segregation of jobs is also persistent; many jobs are stereotyped as "male" or "female"; fully two-thirds of men or women would have to change occupations for their distributions across occupations to be similar. Social science literature has established a correlation between average occupational wage levels and the extent of female representation in the occupation: the more a job is done by women, the lower its average wage level. It is this connection between "femaleness" and lower wage levels that is challenged by the comparable worth strategy. Comparable worth advocates believe that the lower wage rates of female jobs are the result at least partly of discrimination and that wage rates should therefore be realigned. The comparable worth strategy generally involves examination of the relative wage rates of jobs held predominantly by women and those held predominantly by men and study of the bases of these wage rates. Via job evaluation procedures, which attempt to establish objective criteria for such job features as skill, effort, responsibility, and working conditions, the relative value of jobs is established and wage rates are realigned accordingly. The general goal of a comparable worth strategy is pay equity—equitable occupational wage rates that are not influenced by the sex, race, or ethnicity of the incumbents.

Comparable worth claims are being raised by workers and their representatives through legislation, collective bargaining, litigation, and other means.[2] Much of the legislative activity occurring at state and local levels is directed at state and municipal civil service systems; comparable worth studies, task forces, and implementation efforts are being undertaken in many jurisdictions (Reichenberg, 1983; Bureau of National Affairs, 1984; National Committee on Pay Equity et al., 1984). With respect to federal law, in 1981 the U.S. Supreme Court in *Gunther* v. *County of Washington* (101 S. Ct. 2242) seemed to open a door for comparable worth claims when it held that a claim of sex-based wage discrimination in dissimilar jobs could be heard under Title VII of the Civil Rights Act of 1964. And recently, in *AFSCME* v. *State of Washington* (578 F. Supp. 846), a federal district court held that the state of Washington must pay wages for state civil service jobs in accordance with the jobs' worth as measured by a study commissioned by the state. Many comparable worth claims are being addressed to very large employers with rather bureaucratic personnel systems that establish pay rates for jobs according to a variety of administrative criteria. Nearly all claims are addressed to single employers and are concerned with an employer's job assignment and wage-setting practices.[3]

---

[2] For more thorough histories of the comparable worth issue, see Treiman and Hartmann (1981), Cain (1985), and a special issue of *Public Personnel Management* on comparable worth (Reichenberg, 1983).

[3] For a discussion of the nature of comparable worth claims, see Hartmann (1984).

Nearly every aspect of the comparable worth strategy would benefit from further scholarly examination: the causes of the pay gàp and of sex segregation in the labor market; the wage determination process; the influence of discrimination in the establishment of the relative wage levels of jobs and occupations; job evaluation methodology; and the implementation of wage realignment. The scientific basis for much of the current activity is at present incomplete. *Women, Work, and Wages: Equal Pay for Jobs of Equal Value* (Treiman and Hartmann, 1981), a report of the National Research Council, requested by the Equal Employment Opportunity Commission (EEOC) to provide guidance on the comparable worth issue, points out that much further research needs to be done. On the basis of a variety of evidence, the report of the NRC Committee on Occupational Classification and Analysis concludes that discrimination affects wage rates and that, in particular, the pay rates of women's jobs are lower than they would be in the absence of discrimination. Precise estimates of how much occupational wage rates are affected by discrimination, however, are difficult to develop and generally unavailable. The measurement of discrimination, the nature of the wage determination process, and the operation of labor markets are currently subjects of some controversy in economics as well as in other social sciences and require further investigation.

Although comparable worth claims generally rely on job evaluation systems to establish the relative worth of jobs, the NRC committee report points out that relatively little research has been done on job evaluation techniques since job evaluation systems were first adopted in the 1930s and 1940s. Now widely used by large enterprises in both the public and private sectors, job evaluation consists of a formal set of procedures for hierarchically ordering jobs on the basis of their relative skill, effort, responsibility, and working conditions for the purpose of establishing relative pay rates. The NRC committee evaluated the desirability of using existing job evaluation plans to determine job worth in pay equity disputes (Treiman, 1979; Treiman and Hartmann, 1981), concluding that: (1) judgments about the content of jobs are highly subjective, (2) the method for choosing and weighting compensable factors in job evaluation schemes tends to perpetuate existing wage disparities between jobs held mainly by women and those held mainly by men, and (3) the existence of multiple job evaluation plans within the same firm makes comparisons of the worth of jobs in different sectors of the firm difficult. Despite these reservations, the committee concluded that job evaluation can be useful in identifying and correcting existing wage discrepancies within firms. In addition to recommending close scrutiny of existing job evaluation plans as well as additional research on the psychometric foundations of job evaluation procedures, the committee proposed strategies that employers might use to remove any discriminatory effects found in plans they currently use (Treiman and Hartmann, 1981:Ch. 4).

Although the committee generally concluded that the comparable worth strategy merited serious consideration as a remedy for wage discrimination, it also pointed out that it had undertaken no examination of implementing comparable worth strategies or of their economic and social consequences. For example, would there be disemployment effects as a result of raising the wages of nurses and secretaries relative to other wage rates? Would changes in the relative wages of different occupations be temporary or long-lasting? What would be the economic consequences for firms? Would firms that raise the wage rates of women's jobs suffer financially? What would be the effect on the total economy? Would there be strong inflationary effects? In addition to possible unknown economic effects, the implementation of comparable worth policies may have far-reaching social effects, altering perceptions of men and women, self-esteem, behavior, job choices, and so forth. From a policy point of view, the costs and benefits of a comparable worth strategy would be illuminated by a comparison with other equal employment opportunity and affirmative action strategies.

Comparable worth strategies do not address all forms of discrimination that may be present in the labor market. Focused on whatever discriminatory element there is in the relative wage rates of jobs within a single employer, it offers no remedy to ensure equal access to all occupations and all workplaces, some of which are more desirable than others; equal promotional opportunities; equal access to job training or educational programs; and so on. Comparable worth policies may well affect how these other, more traditional equal employment opportunity policies function and may help or hinder achievement of their goals. In this context it should be pointed out that the concept of comparable worth is as relevant to the relative wage rates of jobs held disproportionately by minority groups as it is to "women's jobs." To the extent that "minority jobs" exist and their wage levels are influenced by race-based wage discrimination, remedies using the comparable worth approach would apply. The wage levels of jobs that are held predominantly by minority women may be even more depressed by discrimination. Virtually no examination of the effect of race or ethnic discrimination on the relative wage levels of jobs has been undertaken, however.

Research Issues

Two general themes and, within these, six major topics emerged from the seminar discussions and hence structure this agenda of needed research.

It is clear that research is needed first on occupational wage differentials and discrimination, including their underlying causes. We need to understand a good deal better than we do now how wages are set and what factors lead to wage differentials in order to decide, both in general and in particular instances, whether and to what extent wage discrimination affects the relative average wage rates of jobs and occupations. It bears stressing at the outset that, in the view of the seminar participants, issues related to wage determination require a multidisciplinary approach. Economics, sociology, and anthropology in particular offer relevant perspectives and methodologies.

Within this general area three specific research topics were identified:

1. We need to understand better how wages are set within enterprises and how they are affected by other employer practices, such as job assignment, as well as by workers' decisions. Although many assumptions are made about the impact of market forces and competition on wage-setting processes within organizations, little research on wage determination within firms has been undertaken.

2. Additional work is needed on the behavior of workers within the labor market. Despite a great deal of research to date, there is still no consensus on the relative importance of choices made by workers, particularly choices made by women workers, regarding investment in human capital; assumptions made by employers regarding women's labor force commitment; and still other factors that help to produce gender differentials in occupational status and earnings.

3. A relatively neglected topic, perhaps because it is taken for granted, is the set of underlying cultural assumptions and belief systems that structure people's attitudes regarding appropriate pay levels for men's and women's jobs and appropriate work for women and men. How does our culture come to value certain kinds of work, or work done by certain kinds of people, more (or less) than other work?

The second major research area identified is wage adjustment strategies and their impact. If comparable worth is adopted as public policy, we need to determine effective ways to implement the policy and to minimize any adverse impact. In contrast to research on some aspects of wage differentials and labor markets, this general area has received very little attention from the social science research community. Three topics were identified:

1. Ways need to be devised to measure the relative worth of jobs. Since existing job evaluation procedures appear to be the principal available method, attention needs to be devoted to improving job evaluation procedures and modifying them to make them appropriate for the assessment of pay discrimination. In particular, the extent of social judgment bias in existing job evaluation systems needs to be assessed and, if it is substantial, eliminated.

2. The economic and other consequences of implementing comparable

worth, and in particular the relative impact of various implementation strategies, need to be assessed. The costs and benefits of the comparable worth
strategy need to be compared with those of other equal employment opportunity and affirmative action strategies. Almost nothing is known to date about
such questions, although they are crucial in assessing the desirability of
alternative policies.

3. Similarly, research is needed on the political aspects of the process of
implementing controversial policies such as comparable worth. Issues such
as consensus building, power relations in the workplace, and negotiating
and other strategies are relevant to how comparable worth policies are
implemented and with what effect. What strategies are likely to be most
effective and to result in the most desirable policy decisions? Examples of
the implementation of comparable worth remedies that come about because
of court orders, laws, or collective bargaining need to be assessed for their
effectiveness in achieving the desired goals.

The seminar participants took a broad view of the research needed to
better understand comparable worth. Such research clearly requires a multidisciplinary approach and the input of experts from several social science
disciplines: psychology, anthropology, sociology, economics, and political
science. The participants did not attempt to set priorities for the research
topics suggested. It is likely that each discipline will view priorities somewhat differently. In the following, research topics with more immediate
practical application to issues of comparable worth implementation are discussed in the section immediately below, "Research on Comparable Worth
and Other Wage Adjustment Strategies." Those that aim more at the underlying causes of what is observed in the labor market today are discussed in the
second major section, "Research on Wage Determinants and Wage Discrimination."

RESEARCH ON COMPARABLE WORTH AND
OTHER WAGE ADJUSTMENT STRATEGIES

Social Judgments, Social Judgment Biases,
and Job Evaluation Procedures

The NRC Committee on Occupational Classification and Analysis concluded that formal job evaluation procedures are a potentially useful tool for
identifying and correcting instances of wage discrimination (Treiman and
Hartmann, 1981). These procedures are increasingly being used as a standard for assessing the comparable worth of jobs, in the context of various
attempts, including litigation, to revise wage structures and eliminate pay
differences based on gender.

Given the application of job evaluation procedures to this new task, these procedures have again come under close technical scrutiny for the first time since they were first developed nearly 50 years ago. The psychometric bases of many of these procedures have been shown to be flawed, and a variety of problematic features have been identified, particularly those associated with social judgment biases (Treiman, 1979; Treiman and Hartmann, 1981:Ch. 4; McArthur, in this volume).

To the extent that job evaluation plans can be used to uncover and correct pay discrimination within firms, more systematic implementation of existing job evaluation systems can help to reduce the male-female earnings gap. However, to the extent that job evaluation systems produce fallible measures of the worth of jobs, they are likely to underestimate the discriminatory portion of the wage gap, for reasons discussed below. Hence, it is likely that a greater reduction of the gap could be achieved by eliminating the problems of measurement error and bias existing in current job evaluation schemes. It is in this role that the social sciences can be most useful.

Industrial psychologists approach the problem of bias existing in job evaluation systems at the level of measurement, since it is at that level that one can investigate the role that social judgments play in introducing bias into the evaluation of the worth of jobs.[4] As discussed below, there are three junctures in the use of job evaluation as a comparable worth strategy at which social judgments can introduce bias: deriving job descriptions, determining a set of compensable factors and the weighting assigned to these factors, and evaluating the worth of jobs with respect to identified compensable factors.

Job Descriptions

Job evaluation systems depend on the ability of raters to describe adequately and fairly the tasks required for incumbents in jobs. Descriptions given by job incumbents, their supervisors, and expert raters of the qualifications required to perform particular jobs tend to be substantially similar. Given the inherently subjective nature of the process, however, job descriptions are vulnerable to systematic errors and biases resulting from stereotyping. Thus, to the extent that women's jobs are undervalued or seen as less responsible as a result of cultural stereotyping, job descriptions of women's jobs may be affected by expectancy bias and may not adequately reflect the abilities required to perform necessary job tasks.

---

[4] This and the following sections rely heavily on the papers by McArthur and Schwab in this volume.

"Halo effects" and availability bias may also affect job descriptions. These effects occur when the same aspects of jobs are salient enough to affect one's perception of other aspects (halo effects) and when some of the most available or easily remembered information affects the perception of other aspects. The job descriptions may also reflect self-enhancement bias, since incumbents often enhance the amount of skill and ability needed for their own jobs. This is a particularly difficult problem in the comparable worth context, since research tentatively suggests that men are more likely than women to enhance descriptions of their abilities (McArthur, in this volume).

Research questions that need to be addressed in the area of job descriptions include the following:

• Are there sex differences in the degree of self-enhancement in job descriptions?

• Under what circumstances and with respect to what attributes of jobs are descriptions by incumbents, supervisors, and experts most likely to differ?

• How much agreement is there between raters as to how they describe jobs?

• Does the degree of inter-rater agreement vary for incumbents, supervisors, and experts?

• Are open-ended descriptions, checklists, or other techniques most likely to produce reliable results?

• How does cultural stereotyping affect job descriptions? Are jobs perceived similarly when they are done by women and by men? Specifically, are responsibility and training time requirements downgraded in descriptions of jobs done mainly by women relative to objectively similar jobs performed mainly by men? What about other attributes of jobs?

Compensable Factors and Weighting

Although existing quantitative job evaluation systems vary in their details, they tend to share certain basic features. A set of attributes of jobs, called compensable factors, is designated and points are assigned to defined levels of each factor. For example, a factor of supervisory responsibility might be designated and a specified number of points assigned depending on the number of people supervised. Each job is evaluated or rated with respect to each of the compensable factors and points assigned. The points for each of the compensable factors are added up, and the total becomes the job worth or job evaluation score for the job in question. These total scores are then used to create a hierarchy of job worth, which is used, sometimes alone and sometimes with other information, to determine the pay rate for each job.

As is evident from this description, the relative ranking of jobs is heavily dependent on which attributes of jobs are designated as compensable factors and how much weight each factor is assigned (see Treiman, 1984a, for a discussion of this specific point). Historically, factors and factor weights have been chosen to maximize the prediction of existing pay rates, by capturing the implicit policy underlying a firm's existing pay structure. The difficulty with this approach, however, is that it has the effect of incorporating any existing gender bias in wages and salaries (see Treiman and Hartmann, 1981:Ch. 4, for further discussion of this point). Even when factors and factor weights are chosen de novo, there is the possibility that traditional cultural stereotypes as to what is valued enter into the choice of compensable factors or the relative weight accorded various factors or both. For example, are coordinating activities, which tend to be characteristic of jobs performed mainly by women, identified as a compensable factor, and, if so, what is its weight relative to that of direct supervision, which tends to be characteristic of jobs performed mainly by men? Is being subjected to constant interruptions identified as an "unfavorable working condition" comparable to working under noisy conditions?

Specific research questions on this topic include the following:

• What criteria are used for identifying compensable factors for existing job evaluation systems?

• Does consensus exist across workers (and management) as to what job factors should be compensated? Does this consensus vary by sex?

• Can job evaluation systems be developed by attempting to capture an underlying consensual basis for making equity judgments across jobs? (See Schwab, in this volume, for more discussion.)

• Are there potential compensable factors in women's work that are not now recognized as legitimate bases for pay differentials? Are there legitimate bases for pay differentials that can be identified over and above the traditional factors of skill, effort, responsibility, and working conditions? Are the compensable factors commonly used in job evaluation plans more relevant for men's jobs than for those of women, so that men's jobs tend to be more favorably rated?

Evaluation of Jobs With Respect to Compensable Factors

Evaluating the worth of jobs with respect to compensable factors is the final stage of the job evaluation process, and it too is subject to social judgment biases. There is preliminary evidence that, other things being equal, prestigious jobs or those with high salaries are rated more highly on compensable factors than lower-prestige and lower-paying jobs (McArthur, in this volume; Schwab, in this volume). This labeling bias is thus likely to result in overestimation of the worth of traditionally male jobs relative to those jobs held mainly by women. Psychologists view this labeling bias as one illustration of halo effects. As they operate in the present context, halo effects refer to the fact that positive or negative characteristics of jobs may bias the evaluation of other attributes. Thus, to the extent that information on the salary or prestige of jobs is available to raters, their evaluation of jobs with respect to compensable factors may be biased. In contrast, preliminary evidence also suggests that the sex composition of jobs does not affect raters' evaluations (Schwab, in this volume).

Availability biases affect the evaluation of jobs with respect to compensable factors as well as initial job descriptions. In this kind of bias, ratings may be affected by the job characteristics most easily remembered. Thus, to the extent that sex stereotyping is a salient characteristic of a job, job dimensions most in line with sex-role stereotypes (e.g., nurturance or compassion in female jobs) will be the most easily remembered.

Research in the area of evaluating jobs with respect to compensable factors should include two important issues:

1. Additional research is needed on whether, and if so how, the salary, prestige, and sex composition of jobs affect the evaluation of jobs with respect to compensable factors.
2. To investigate availability and expectancy biases, researchers should have job descriptions evaluated by several different raters with the order of job dimensions varied; ways to reduce the possible negative effects of stereotyping on rating should be explored.

More generally, we need studies of the overall effectiveness of reformed job evaluation plans: How effective are various improvements in job evaluation systems in making them more useful tools in comparable worth cases? The effects of statistical adjustments to correct for the bias in weights based on market wage rates and of improvements in eliminating any gender bias from job descriptions and rating judgments are particular areas for examination.

The Economic Consequences of Implementing Comparable Worth

This case [*Lemons* v. *City and County of Denver*, known as the Denver nurses' case] . . . is pregnant with the possibility of disrupting the entire economic system of the United States of America. . . . What Dr. Bardwell [witness for the plaintiff] is saying is that I should open the Pandora's Box . . . of restructuring the entire economy of the United States of America. I am not going to do it. . . . It would be completely disruptive of our

way of life. . . . The overall result here, in my judgment, would be absolute chaos in the economy of the United States of America if any such program ever [were] adopted.
                    Decision of Fred M. Winner, April 28, 1978
                    620 F.2d 228 (10th Cir.), cert. denied, 449 U.S. 888 (1980)

Currently there is virtually no research on whether the implementation of a comparable worth policy would contribute to the elimination of discrimination from the U.S. labor market; there is also virtually no research investigating the effects on the U.S. economy of instituting such a policy. Judge Winner, in the quotation above, reflected the concern of many business leaders and others when he stated that implementing comparable worth would have disastrous consequences for our economic system. While there is currently no empirical evidence to support this assertion, there is also a lack of evidence for the contrary claim that comparable worth would have *no* negative consequences. Moreover, little detailed consideration has been given to strategies for adjusting pay rates according to comparable worth criteria, or to the consequences of alternative pay adjustment strategies (see, however, the discussion of statistical adjustments to achieve pay equity in Treiman and Hartmann, 1981:Ch. 4). Various alternatives have been suggested, including raising the salaries of low-paying, women's jobs to the average level of salaries for comparable men's jobs in the same enterprise, lowering the salaries of men's jobs to equal those of comparable women's jobs, or, perhaps more realistically, raising the salaries of low-paying jobs at a faster rate than those of higher-paid jobs (a strategy used in Sweden, which has instituted a policy of higher proportional wage increases for those at the bottom of the wage hierarchy). The costs and benefits of comparable worth strategies also need to be compared with other equal employment opportunity and affirmative action policies, which have the same end goal of eliminating discrimination from the labor market but attack different parts of the problem and use different means with likely differing consequences.

What sort of economic and noneconomic consequences would flow from each intervention strategy? In this context, it is important to delineate types of consequences in order to assess whether such effects are significant. For example, does instituting a comparable worth strategy increase inflation and, if so, by how much? Alternatively, if employers are required to pay higher salaries, they may compensate by not offering as many jobs, thus leading to disemployment. If so, how much disemployment would result? Assuming that women workers currently bear the financial cost of wage discrimination because of their location in low-paid employment, would such a cost be reallocated to other workers if comparable worth were adopted? Which workers would bear the brunt of any such consequences?

How do these costs differ from the costs imposed by other equal employment opportunity and affirmative action policies?

In a theoretical discussion of likely effects of implementing various comparable worth strategies, Bergmann (in this volume) speculates that wage realignment achieved by cutting salaries of (the mostly male) workers in high-paying jobs might result in substantial turnover. If, however, realignment were achieved by raising the salaries of low-paid (mostly female) jobs, firms would have to contend with an increase in payroll costs. Alternatively, firms could choose to increase the salaries of incumbents in low-paid jobs at a higher percentage rate than incumbents in high-paid employment, thereby reducing the likelihood of higher turnover and payroll costs. Killingsworth (in this volume), in contrast, argues that implementing comparable worth would result in increases in unemployment and disemployment, resulting in a reduction in output and an increase in consumer prices.

There are at present no realistic scenarios of the economic effects of adopting this form of pay equity, and there is also a lack of agreement regarding what little evidence exists on the effects of instituting a comparable worth policy. The Australian experience is a prime case in point. In 1972 the Australian Federal Tribunal established a policy of equal pay for work of equal value. Ratner (1980) reports that once this policy was implemented in 1975 the earnings of women who worked full time increased 30 percent relative to those of their male counterparts. Moreover, some (Ratner, 1980; Gregory and Duncan, 1981) argue that the policy had no deleterious effects, while others (Killingsworth, in this volume) argue that institution of the policy increased unemployment and decreased job growth for women.

In large measure, whether a comparable worth policy would have adverse employment and inflation effects depends on how much effect discrimination has had in establishing the relative wages of male and female jobs and how much comparable worth wage adjustments correct (or possibly overcorrect) for those effects. That is, economists generally believe that eliminating discrimination in pay rates would eventually lead to a more efficient, and more economically beneficial, allocation and utilization of human resources. Resources that are incorrectly priced are incorrectly used; the general tendency is to use too little of an overpriced resource and too much of an underpriced one. When prices are corrected, resources find their most productive use. Thus, while in the short run there might be dislocations of various kinds, in the long run, as resource reallocation occurred, eliminating wage discrimination would not be expected to cause either inflation or unemployment. There is a serious question, however, about whether comparable worth policies provide a useful means of contributing to the ultimate goal of a discrimination-free labor market or whether other, more established policies, such as enforcement of Title VII, Title IX, and other sections of the Civil Rights Act of 1964, are sufficient or possibly more effective in the long run (see Killingsworth, in this volume).

To estimate the economic consequences of the implementation of comparable worth strategies, a better understanding is needed of the extent of likely wage changes, their relationship to discrimination, various implementation or alternative strategies, and differential impacts on various groups of workers. This research area encompasses a number of important issues:

• Labor market simulations of wage changes of the sort that would result from the implementation of comparable worth strategies could shed light on the likely effects of such changes on employment levels in different occupations and on inflation or other macroeconomic phenomena. Simulations of discrimination-free labor markets, and resulting hypothetical wage rates and levels of employment in various occupations, could be used for comparison.

• It is important to identify and estimate the extent of the economic effects of comparable worth strategies, particularly wage, price, and employment effects, and determine which groups of workers, employers, and consumers will be affected and how the effects will develop over time. Such research should include consideration of whether and how much employers might benefit from restructuring work, reduced turnover, increased satisfaction, and increased worker quality as well as the obvious costs; it should consider the extent of possible societywide benefits (such as higher incomes and reduced poverty) as well as the obvious issues of inflation and unemployment. What will be the net effect of comparable worth policies on national income distribution?

• We need realistic scenarios of the financial cost to employers of implementing various comparable worth strategies. Such scenarios could be based on case studies of employers such as the city of San Jose and the state of Washington, where comparable worth policies have been implemented: What benefits accrue to firms and workers? Are job structures and career ladders rearranged? Do inequities reassert themselves following intervention?

• Comparisons are needed of the costs and benefits of comparable worth strategies and other equal employment opportunity and affirmative action strategies. How successful have other strategies been? Have they been used sufficiently?

The Process of Implementing Comparable Worth

Comparable worth is a political as well as an economic issue. The courts, various state and federal legislative bodies, employers, employees, and unions are all involved in a complex process of building consensus, negotiating strategies, and developing policy with respect to the implementation of comparable worth as a pay strategy. The reason for all this political activity is the persistent wage gap between men and women. Various sections of this report propose further research on hypothesized explanations for the earnings differential (e.g., supply-side or demand-side explanations), ways to improve the efficiency of job evaluation systems (e.g., by eliminating social judgment biases), and the consequences of implementing a comparable worth strategy (e.g., on disemployment or inflation). In this section we turn to a different set of research issues—how interested parties reconcile their separate values in solving pay problems in the workplace (Remick and Steinberg, 1984).

The inherently political nature of comparable worth can be seen most clearly in the politicization of job evaluation. Job evaluation was, prior to the late 1970s, merely a set of formalized procedures used within firms for purposes of establishing pay rates for jobs. Few people other than industrial psychologists and personnel specialists gave much thought to the intricacies of various job evaluation plans in use in U.S. industries. Collett (1983:325) best sums up the important political role that job evaluation has come to play in recent years:

Personnel professions should give thanks that because of "comparable worth" the process of evaluating positions and determining their monetary value has been raised from the level of technicians, arguing over "system" approaches, to the level of executives and legislative bodies, deciding policy issues. This is because they have been forced by determined women to consider more than traditional technical factors in wage determination as they have been told that traditional factors do not truly represent a nondiscriminatory basis for evaluating the work of employees in cross-occupational comparisons.

While job evaluation plans are based on assumptions about rational economic behavior, in establishing pay rates managers must also respond to ongoing social dynamics within organizations (Rosenbaum, in this volume). With the growing use of job evaluation systems in comparable worth contexts, the adoption of any plan depends on its credibility with various groups in the workplace—the pay rates set for jobs must satisfy management, employees, and labor unions. Job evaluation plans instituted in organizations must thus satisfy perceptions of internal equity (i.e., jobs seen as comparable should be paid equivalent wages). With respect to comparable worth, job evaluation plans would be viewed as credible to the extent that gender is not a compensable factor. Factors that are compensated need to be directly and demonstrably job-related.

One implication of these developments is that successful implementation of job evaluation as a comparable worth strategy may require participation of all the various constituent groups—management, workers, and their representatives. The benefit of such full participation in the process of devising or selecting job evaluation systems, other than the obvious one of enhancing perceptions of internal equity, is that scrutiny of pay plans would make their bases for pay (as well as their implicit value structures) more explicit. Plans open to such scrutiny would enable workers and management alike to identify and correct specific instances of pay inequity. A growing number of firms have begun this process of developing job evaluation plans jointly through management and union negotiation, including AT&T (through its Joint Union-Management Occupational Job Evaluation Committee) and the Communications Workers of America (Hartmann and Treiman, 1984)—although the reorganization of AT&T has slowed the process.

While comparable worth has received the most attention in recent years, it is not the only strategy that has pay equity as a goal. Breaking down occupational segregation by sex in the U.S. occupational structure is an alternative approach, although such segregation has proven quite resistant to change; the role of affirmative action is particularly important in eliminating sex segregation (Reskin and Hartmann, 1985). Implementing comparable worth thus requires investigation of the effect this policy would have on alternative strategies, such as efforts at job integration and affirmative action. In addition, the effects of comparable worth policies on other established wage negotiation mechanisms, such as management-union relations, need to be investigated.

In light of these concerns, there are a number of researchable issues:

• How is consensus among groups with different interests reached in identifying compensable factors for job evaluation systems? In defining internal equity? In defining criteria for weighting compensable factors?

• What strategies for consensus building and negotiation would work best in reaching consensus on equity issues?

• How do joint management-worker groups affect the implementation of comparable worth strategies?

• What implications does implementing comparable worth in an organization have for affirmative action programs? For union activity?

• What effect might race, ethnic, or regional differences have on implementation strategies?

• Exploratory case studies of organizations in which comparable worth is instituted could shed light on how implementation proceeds and on what problems emerge.

• Assessments are needed of the success of comparable worth remedies that are now in effect or that may be ordered by the courts or negotiated by unions and management. Do the remedies achieve the desired goals? Why or why not?

RESEARCH ON WAGE DETERMINANTS AND WAGE DISCRIMINATION

Pay-Setting Practices and Pay Differentials Within Organizations

The pay and salary levels of different jobs within an enterprise are not automatically determined by the operation of abstract forces such as "the market" or "low valuation of women's work." They are rather the result of decisions made by individuals on an ongoing basis as they incorporate their perceptions and experience of market requirements, their beliefs and prejudices, and so on. These decisions are poorly understood, partly because it is difficult for researchers to obtain access to data on individual firms. Hence, a host of questions on pay-setting practices and pay differentials, and on the impact of such practices and differentials on the gender gap in average pay, remain unanswered. In reviewing these questions in more detail, it is useful to divide them into two categories: (1) What practices determine access to desirable jobs and in particular limit the access of women workers to such jobs? (2) How are pay rates for different jobs determined and what factors determine lower pay for jobs held mainly by women?

Job Access

One of the major reasons that women tend to earn less on average than men in the same enterprise is that women and men tend to hold different jobs, with women disproportionately concentrated in the low-paying jobs while men are in the high-paying jobs. While it has been recognized for some time that the level of occupational sex segregation in the labor force is high, the full extent of gender segregation within enterprises has not been clear until recent work by Bielby and Baron (1984a, 1984b). Using data from a sample of establishments in California, Bielby and Baron (1984b) found nearly complete job segregation by sex. In more than half the establishments they investigated, job classifications were completely segregated by sex and in only one-fifth were indices of segregation less than 90, meaning that 90 percent of the women (or men) would have to change jobs to have an occupational distribution identical to that of men (or women). Workplace segregation can take many forms. Complete job segregation occurs when firms hire only men or only women for particular jobs or when men and women are hired to do the same work but are given different job titles. Even when jobs are integrated, workplace segregation often occurs because men and women in the same job titles are segregated spatially or because men and women deal only with clients of the same sex.

Bielby and Baron (1984b) identify several determinants of this substantial job and workplace segregation. First, sex biases appear to exist in the allocation of women and men to job ladders within firms, with men being assigned to longer and better-paid job ladders and women to truncated ladders. (However, we know very little about promotion ladders, specifically, about the length of promotion chains, the average length of service at each level in the chain, the probability of skipping steps, and so forth.) Second, part of this sex-specific job assignment is the result of former legal restrictions on how much women can be required to lift. While these weight restrictions were eliminated in 1970, the institutionalization of such workplace practices as well as bureaucratic inertia means that differential assignment by sex in manufacturing jobs persists. Third, organizational scale is strongly associated with sex segregation: larger workplaces have greater levels of sex segregation. Increasing organizational scale leads to the implementation of rationalized and bureaucratized personnel practices, rules, and procedures that operate, often with the sanction of collective bargaining agreements, to institutionalize and hence perpetuate workplace segregation. These findings suggest that organizational mechanisms may operate to sustain job and workplace segregation at such a level that women may seldom work in the same job as their male counterparts.

Although we know that job segregation contributes to the male-female pay gap, we know little about the mechanisms that cause increasing proportions of women in a job to be associated with lower earnings. Knowing more about the mechanisms that lead to job segregation within firms will tell us more about the motivations of employers and workers and the extent to which intentional discrimination affects their behavior. If discrimination is a factor in assignment, it may also be a factor in the setting of relative wage rates of jobs. Segregationist attitudes and practices of employers also affect the supply of and demand for workers of various sexes in various jobs. Answers to a number of research questions are needed in this area:

- What makes some jobs male in some workplaces but female in others (e.g., waiters, hairdressers)?
- Which workplace practices tend to perpetuate job segregation by sex? For example, to what extent are gender differences built into the structure of jobs? Do women move up within "female" tracks and men in "male" tracks? Which practices tend to reduce sex segregation?
- Which jobs have been successfully integrated? Do they remain so?
- How does sex segregation affect the relative wage rates of men's and women's jobs?

Pay-Setting Practices

In addition to the mechanisms described above that tend to perpetuate workplace segregation, compensation systems within firms often set lower salaries for occupations held mainly by women than for those held mainly by men. According to economic theory, differential salaries are attributable both to differences in demand for certain jobs and to the differing amounts of availability of labor. Hence, those jobs most in demand and facing the most severe labor shortages should command the highest salaries. Yet pay scales often seem relatively unresponsive to market forces. The nursing profession is a case in point. Despite shortages of nurses in recent years, nursing salaries have not increased substantially relative to other salaries. Instead, hospitals have used nonwage forms of competition to attract nurses (offering one-time bonuses, recruiting nurses from abroad, and so forth). Hospitals also rarely differentiate different nursing specialities in compensation (Remick, 1984). Case studies of salary-setting practices in hospitals would thus be very illuminating.

For people employed in large organizations in the private sector and in public institutions, wages are likely to be determined by institutionalized procedures. Thus, for a large segment of the U.S. work force, job salaries are a function of intraorganizational wage-setting practices that may adjust only slowly, if at all, to changes in the supply and demand for labor outside the firm or agency. Many large firms organize their internal labor markets into career ladders; they often promote from within and may have unique demands for labor that they supply with their own workers. Relative wage rates also reflect the values of management and must be responsive to employee perceptions of equity within an organization.

More generally, there is a strong need for additional organizational case studies of the kind Rosenbaum (in this volume) reports. Such studies would help us better understand how wages are actually set within enterprises. Specifically, we need to know more about the use of formal or informal job evaluation procedures; the ways in which job evaluation results are used in the wage-setting process; the ways market wages are taken into account through surveys and other means; whether, to what extent, and under what circumstances wages are adjusted to reflect market forces; the role of management-labor negotiations in the way wages are set for specific jobs; and, finally, what kinds of seniority rules, shift differentials, and bonuses exist for which kinds of jobs. Ideally such information would be available for a representative sample of enterprises, so that it would be possible to understand variations in the wage-setting process for enterprises in different sectors. Analysis of this kind would go a long way toward helping us understand the role of organizations in creating and perpetuating pay differences between women and men.

A research agenda in the area of intraorganizational practices affecting compensation would include investigation into both the determinants of workplace segregation (discussed above) and wage-setting practices within organizations. One way to approach these issues would be to study how wage structures are developed in new occupations, industries, and organizations. Are wage structures (i.e., job hierarchies with respect to worth) established de novo or do they mimic hierarchies already existing in other organizations? Most important, does sex typing of new jobs or occupations occur before or after wage assignment? Other questions for research include the following:

• How are surveys of salaries and wages in other firms used by employers in the wage determination process? What other mechanisms are there for "market forces" to enter into a firm's wage-setting practices?

• Are some firms relatively insulated from market forces in setting their wage rates? How does degree of insulation vary by size of firm, region, industry, occupation, size, and so on?

• To what extent are other employers in local labor markets affected by the wage-setting practices of large organizations?

• Are there any strategies used at the organizational level to adjust the internal wage hierarchy produced by existing job evaluation systems to take into account changes in supply and demand or other factors?

• Do newly developed job evaluation systems tend to incorporate traditional values? To respond to current market conditions?

• What would occupational wage levels be in the absence of sex-based wage discrimination? In the absence of other forms of employment discrimination as well?

• What have been the effects of significant influxes of women into traditionally male jobs (or men into traditionally female jobs) on the status and the wage rates associated with those jobs (e.g., lawyers, doctors, bus drivers, bakers)?

Occupational Choice, Careers, and Work Histories

In the previous section we noted the very substantial segregation of men and women into different jobs within enterprises. Much of that within-firm segregation reflects occupational segregation (and, as we noted, some of it is firm-specific segregation even of integrated occupations). Considering the labor force as a whole, there is a strong tendency for men and women to work at entirely different occupations.[5] Women are concentrated in nursing, school teaching, retail sales, clerical work, a variety of service occupations, and some factory jobs, in particular those involving hand-assembly; moreover, most workers in these occupations and jobs are women. In contrast, many professions and managerial occupations, most non-retail-sales occupations, and almost all craft and laboring occupations are performed mainly by men. For some of these occupations people train in advance and seek employment in the area of their training; for other occupations people are likely to be assigned by employers. There is substantial disagreement among researchers as to whether the extent of occupational segregation results mainly from discriminatory factors or mainly from the choice of individual workers. The research issue is concerned with determining to what extent women choose to supply themselves to jobs with low wages as opposed to their being denied equivalent access to higher-paying male employment. Thus, the interest is in distinguishing between choice and constraint as explanations for why women are concentrated disproportionately in low-paying jobs (leaving aside for the moment the possibility that jobs pay poorly because women do them).

Arguments based on the human capital perspective in economics generally hold that men and women have different "tastes" for employment (see Marini and Brinton, 1984, for a review of these arguments). According to this view, because they anticipate greater family responsibilities, women choose less demanding jobs or choose to invest less in education and on-the-job training; hence they are less able to compete with men for high-paying employment. Men's greater earnings are also seen as deriving from their greater work experience and more stable work history. The assumption is that a woman's marital and childbearing responsibilities disrupt her labor force continuity and hence negatively affect her earning power vis-à-vis men.

Alternatives to the human capital approach focus on demand-side factors, arguing that women do not have equal access to high-paying jobs held disproportionately by men because of unequal access to information, training, or the jobs themselves. Theorists accepting this explanation for the male-female earnings gap stress institutional mechanisms that limit access— for example, as we have already noted, job ladders and other intraorganiza-

---

[5] It is useful in discussions of this kind to distinguish between jobs and occupations. *Jobs* are specific positions in specific settings, e.g., professor of sociology at UCLA, driver for Checker Cab Company in Washington, D.C., and so on. There can be one or more persons in each job. *Occupations* are aggregations of jobs requiring similar skills and responsibilities and involving the performance of similar tasks, e.g., college and university professors, sociology; taxi drivers; and so on. Both jobs and occupations can be defined at varying levels of detail or aggregation.

tional mechanisms that limit women's mobility within organizations (see Roos and Reskin, 1984, for an overview).

Outside these two main currents of explanation, additional factors affect the extent of sex segregation. For example, occupational sex segregation is expected to decline somewhat through the remainder of this decade because of the increasing integration of occupations, but anticipated rapid growth of occupations that traditionally have been held by women will prevent its further decline (Beller and Han, 1984). These and other factors affecting occupational sex segregation need further investigation. (For a review of the possible effects of demographic and economic pressures on occupational segregation, see Cain, in this volume; for a general review of what is known about occupational sex segregation, see Reskin and Hartmann, 1985.)

Research in this area can help us weigh the relative importance of choice, training and education, limited access, and so on, in the perpetuation of both occupational segregation and the pay gap. Research topics fall into two broad areas: (1) occupational choice and labor supply and (2) occupational careers and work histories.

Occupational Choice and Labor Supply

Occupational choice and labor supply issues are relatively well covered by ongoing research (see Marini and Brinton, 1984, for an overview). From one perspective, occupational choice and other labor supply explanations for the wage gap concentrate on the characteristics of workers themselves that lead to employment in sex-typical jobs. In this view, sex differences in socialization create sex-specific characteristics of workers, such as occupational preferences or skills. Thus males and females are viewed as developing very different expectations about the type of work they will do, and even about what work is appropriate for them to do, as adults.

Marini and Brinton (1984) provide evidence that occupational aspirations among children are highly sex-typed, so that segregation with respect to aspirations is almost as great as the actual occupational segregation of the employed labor force. Occupational expectations are even more sex-typed than aspirations, suggesting that even when girls aspire to nontraditional employment their expectations tend to be more sex-typical. These differential aspirations and expectations reflect sex-role socialization that occurs in families, in schools, from textbooks and other educational material, from television and other mass media, and through career guidance counselors and vocational education, all of which operate to encourage boys and girls to aspire to sex-traditional employment.

While we know that aspirations and expectations play a role in determining adult occupational attainment, there is little evidence on how important that role is or the process whereby such aspirations translate into attainment. And further research to determine the factors identified by the human capital school, discussed above, is also needed: Do women's expectations about family responsibilities affect their occupational choice? How?

A research agenda in the area of occupational choice would include the following questions:[6]

• What is the relationship between the sex-typing of occupational aspirations (as well as expectations) and attainments? To what extent does sex-typing in occupational aspirations account for sex segregation in employment?

• How do occupational aspirations and expectations change over time?

• To what extent do sex differences in ability, skill, or commitment account for differences in occupational placement?

• How might changes be effected in the labor supply to various jobs? For example, what would be needed to persuade men to enter traditionally female jobs?

• To what extent do people take jobs that are available to them, rather than undergoing an elaborate job search process? To what extent does sex-typing occur at the personnel office rather than because of individual choice?

• How do the policies of the armed services' excluding women from certain occupational specialties affect women's job choices?

• To the extent that marital responsibilities affect women's occupational choices, we would expect women more often than men to choose easy-entry/easy-exit jobs in which skills do not depreciate. To what extent are women more likely than men to work in such jobs?

• To what extent do women and men have specific occupational knowledge about jobs traditionally held by the opposite sex? To what extent does this affect occupational choice? How effective is advertising the pay rates of jobs in increasing the number of women who apply to traditionally male, higher-paying jobs?

• What is known about the influence of demographic and economic pressures on occupational sex segregation and prospects for pay equity? Further research (in the form of simulation models) is needed to assess likely future levels of sex segregation. Specifically, such models should include research on the age structure of the labor force and of occupations, age differences in job and occupational mobility, differences in cohort size, effects of changes in sex composition on occupational wages, training and skill needs, and whether job export and displacement by technology will have differential effects on the pay and employment prospects of men and women.

---

[6] The first three research topics are taken from Marini and Brinton (1984).

Occupational Careers and Work Histories

The relevance of occupational careers and work histories derives from the role of labor force experience in explaining the wage gap between men and women. As described above, most supply-side explanations for the earnings gap make the claim that women's lower earnings relative to men's are attributable in large measure to gender differences in the extent and pattern of work experience. Specifically, the argument is made that women earn less than men do because their participation in the labor force is intermittent and hence their total amount of accumulated experience is low relative to that of their male counterparts. In order to test these expectations, researchers need continuous work history data that describe how men and women organize their work lives. Currently there is available for the United States only one major data set with continuous work histories for men—the 1968 Johns Hopkins Life History Survey of a sample of men ages 30 to 39—and none for women (Treiman, 1984b). The National Longitudinal Surveys of Labor Force Experience provide data on job and occupation changes at fixed points in time for samples of both men and women for several consecutive years. The Panel Study on Income Dynamics provides similar data for a sample of families who have been followed since 1968. Their longitudinal nature makes these samples very valuable, but, because they do not contain continuous work histories, they do not include all job transitions.

What we do know about sex differences in work experience comes from survey data about events at particular points in the socioeconomic life cycle (i.e., first job, current job, job 5 years ago). From such data it is clear that differences in total amount of labor force participation affect women's occupational opportunities (see Treiman, 1984b, for an overview). We also know that the age pattern of women's labor force participation has changed substantially since the turn of the century. Fewer women drop out of the labor force to have children; indeed, among the youngest cohorts of women, practically no dip in labor force participation is observed during the peak childbearing years. To the extent that continuous participation affects occupational mobility, one might expect women's occupational prospects to increase in the future. The problem with this expectation, however, is that current women workers with continuous labor force attachment have an occupational distribution that is very different from that of men. This finding suggests that continuous attachment may not benefit women workers in the same way it does men (see Roos, 1983, for a review and partial test of this proposition).

Some researchers have approached these issues by aggregating individual work histories into job or career trajectories in which the question of interest is the pattern of variation in occupational status or income over the course of the career. Our concern is whether men or women, or women with differing family responsibilities, have similar career trajectories. Although such questions are only now beginning to be addressed, preliminary indications are that women have much flatter occupational status and earnings trajectories than do men (Treiman, 1984b). But the reasons for this are far from being adequately understood. Moreover, studies of this topic implicitly assume that most workers have orderly career progressions, although this has not been empirically established; indeed, available evidence (e.g., Evans and Laumann, 1983) suggests the contrary.

There are many questions for future research in this area:

• Do orderly job trajectories (successive jobs) exist at all and, if so, for what categories of workers?

• Do men and women have different career trajectories? Do men and women with differing levels of family responsibilities differ in their job trajectories?

• To what extent do formal career paths (established by the organization) and informal career paths (the actual pattern followed by individuals) correspond?

• What are the effects of career ladders (or job tracks) on wage assignment? For example, are salaries higher for jobs leading to key parts of the organization?

• What are the patterns of shifts in and across jobs? Will women who have moved into traditionally male jobs remain in these jobs or will they shift into traditionally female jobs?

• What is the role of occupational experience in enhancing earnings? Is experience worth more in some kinds of jobs than in others? Is experience worth more in the sorts of jobs men tend to hold than those women tend to hold?

• How does experience enhance productivity? Is it actually increased productivity that is rewarded, or simply seniority? How does this differ across different sorts of jobs?

• Do labor force experience, occupational experience, and firm-specific experience differ in their impact on earnings? Can such differences help explain gender differences in earnings? Occupational differences in earnings?

Culture: Beliefs About Gender and Jobs

The NRC Committee on Occupational Classification and Analysis (Treiman and Hartmann, 1981) concluded that there is no strictly scientific or technical basis for determining the relative worth of jobs, because "worth" is ultimately a matter of values. (The report noted, however, that once criteria of worth are agreed to, the establishment of job worth hierarchies is amenable to technical solutions.) For this reason, it is important to investigate the varying and competing belief systems underlying the value judgments made about different kinds of jobs and workers. While the centrality of the concepts of worth and value to wages is questioned by economists, who view wages as prices that signal us about the allocation of scarce resources, most economists would acknowledge that cultural beliefs and practices do play a role in wage determination.

There is some evidence that virtually all societies with wage economies value similar attributes of jobs, since the relative prestige of occupations is essentially similar throughout the world and similar attributes of jobs— mainly skill and responsibility—account for their relative prestige (Treiman, 1977). There is also some evidence of consensus within societies regarding what constitutes a "just wage" for different sorts of jobs (Jasso and Rossi, 1977). The available evidence is highly aggregated, however; it refers to very general categories of occupations and to measures such as "prestige" or "just wages" rather than to more specific attributes of value of the kind that would differentiate jobs within individual enterprises. Research is needed on how more generalized cultural beliefs are transformed in workplaces and used as guides in determining wage rates and in assigning "appropriate" jobs to men and women and on what employers and workers value about jobs in specific settings.

With respect to the first issue, the use of generalized cultural beliefs in workplaces, it would be of interest to know if there are "folk" models that people use to justify setting differential wages for traditionally male and female jobs. For example, one very important belief system affecting the setting of pay rates in our society is the equation of the worth of jobs with existing pay rates and the belief that wages are determined largely or solely by the operation of the laws of supply and demand. That in actual practice supply and demand may not always be the determining factors or that many factors such as discrimination affect supply and demand may not alter the underlying belief.

Furthermore, why are the value systems observed in the workplace often contradictory? For example, night work was historically viewed as appropriate for nurses but not for other jobs, in which women were competing more directly with men. What are the factors that led to a shift in values during World War II so that, once women were needed for the war effort as riveters, welders, and other skilled workers, their suitability for such blue-collar skilled work was no longer questioned? Why is it that certain "dirty" jobs traditionally held by men are considered inappropriate for women, particularly for white women—while nursing, which also involves "dirtiness," is not, and other dirty jobs such as cleaning are often associated with minority women?

How do cultural constructions of gender, of what it means to be a man or a woman, affect employers' and workers' notions of appropriate jobs for women and men and appropriate wage levels for those jobs? What role does the widely shared belief that women are and should be primarily responsible for household and family care play' in the labor market? Historians have shown how specific cultural constructions of gender have shaped women's lives and influenced perceptions of women as workers (Cott, 1977; Eisenstein, 1983); similar analyses are needed for the present. In recent years, scholars of labor studies have developed the concept of work culture to describe the set of beliefs and practices that govern interactions at work (Melosh, 1982); work cultures, too, legitimate or challenge current cultural constructions of work appropriate for women and men.

With respect to the second issue—what employers and workers value about jobs in specific settings—it would be of interest to know how such values are formed, what they are, and how they change. Is there consensus that jobs requiring more skill, responsibility, and effort or those performed under difficult or unpleasant conditions deserve more pay? What about specific measures of these attributes? Even if there is consensus that skill should be rewarded, is there agreement that formal education, years of experience required to become highly qualified, specialized knowledge, or other specific indicators are appropriate measures of skill? What about the skills that many women have as a result of caring for families and keeping households running? Are these acknowledged in the workplace? If consensus is lacking with respect to particular classes or measures, is lack of agreement systematic? That is, do employers and employees disagree in systematic ways? Do male and female workers disagree? What about manual and nonmanual workers? In short, we need to know far more than we do now about perceptions of what attributes of jobs should be compensated.

Apart from assumptions about the value of different attributes of jobs, there is reason to believe that pay rates are affected by assumptions about the value of different sorts of workers. Historically in the United States it was considered appropriate to pay blacks less than whites and women less than men for doing the same job. Indeed, until passage of the Equal Pay Act of 1963 and the Civil Rights Act of 1964, such distinctions were often incorporated into law, e.g., lower pay for women being explicitly justified on the grounds that men needed higher pay in order to support their families (Kessler-Harris, 1982; May, 1982). Currently, such overt wage discrimination is illegal, and the wage gap between men and women doing the same work has probably narrowed considerably. Shifting values have now led some groups to argue that women and men should in general earn similar salaries even though they typically work in different types of jobs. It is suggested that "women's work" and women themselves need to be revalued—hence the interest in the comparable worth strategy.

The overall research issue that emerged from deliberations at the Seminar on Comparable Worth Research is the role that underlying belief systems play in the setting of wages, particularly in the explanation of why men's and women's jobs are valued differently. Our proposed research agenda on underlying belief systems focuses on three major topics: (1) What are the varying belief systems that currently influence the wage-setting process? (2) Is the differential evaluation of male and female tasks reflected in the wage-assignment process? If so, how? and (3) How are competing belief systems reflected in existing job evaluation systems?

Existence of Belief Systems

There are several research areas that promise to increase our knowledge of how alternative belief systems may affect the wage-setting process. Questions for research include the following:

• Discourse analysis is a method used by anthropologists, linguists, psychologists, and philosophers of language to investigate verbal or written texts. Would this method usefully uncover the basic assumptions or beliefs about individuals and cultures that underlie the wage-setting process?

• What belief systems underlie workers' occupational choices? For example, do some beliefs lead men to be uninterested in working in jobs in which women predominate?

• Are peoples' judgments about what salaries should be (i.e., deserved salaries) very different from actual salaries (i.e., existing salaries)? How do peoples' judgments about deserved salaries evolve?

• How do ideas based in economics affect people's views of the value of work and the appropriate salaries for people and jobs? Do people's valuations of jobs reflect, for example, their understanding of their relative value to employers based on their productivity? Do they affect their understanding of shortages or excess supply?

• With changes in the technology of work, how will the evaluation of men's and women's work change? Does technology contribute to establishing new bases for consensus about the evaluation of men's and women's jobs?

• Do the assumptions regarding the setting of wages for part-time work differ from those for full-time work? To what extent are part-time salaries lower because employers view incumbents (generally women) in those jobs as secondary workers?

Analysis of Task and Wage Assignment

In addition to knowing what belief systems underlie the wage-setting process, it is important to consider how these belief systems become incorporated into the wage-setting process. In this context, we propose research on the identification of "male" and "female" tasks and a determination of whether such tasks are differentially valued:

• What are the component tasks required in jobs that are perceived as female or male? Are these also sex-typed?
• If tasks are identified as male or female, are male tasks more highly valued? Does adding female tasks (e.g., typing, nurturing, waiting on tables, clerical work) to job descriptions reduce the perceived value of a job?
• Does the established consensus about the worth of tasks in jobs decline if the number of women entering the field increases? Do the tasks change?
• If female tasks or jobs are less positively evaluated, how does this affect the compensation assigned?

Belief Systems and Job Evaluation

Job evaluation systems always embody a particular value system. When a firm adopts a specific job evaluation system, it accepts a particular set of values according to which jobs are hierarchically arrayed. Because job evaluation schemes are used in a large, possibly increasing, number of firms, it is important that researchers investigate the belief systems underlying existing job evaluation plans:

• Is there general societal consensus regarding which attributes of jobs ought to be compensated and regarding the relative importance of various attributes? If not, do workers and management value attributes of jobs differently?
• Do men and women value attributes of jobs differently?
• What belief systems underlie the various job evaluation systems currently in use in U.S. firms? How are these beliefs reflected in the compensable factors and weighting scheme of current systems?

CONCLUSION

Comparable worth claims and strategies for adjusting wages based on such claims need to be understood as part of the larger process of wage determination and as one of several means of wage adjustments. In this context we need to know much more about how wages are actually determined within firms; about how people's attitudes and beliefs influence wages; about how workers' behavior—their job choices, their investment in training—influence their labor market outcomes; and so on. With regard to wage adjustment strategies relevant to comparable worth claims, job evaluation plans are clearly an important element, and a considerable portion of the discussion at the seminar was devoted to research designed to improve job evaluation plans. Equally important, however, are the conditions that lead to the successful implementation of job evaluation plans or other methods of achieving pay equity and the economic consequences of implementing comparable worth policies relative to those of other equal employment opportunity policies.

Some of the research that we suggest represents continuation and extension of already-established research areas (such as research on discrimination, job choice, and work careers), and some represents new departures (the role of cultural beliefs in wage setting) or new directions (job evaluation methodology, consensus building in the workplace). The accomplishment of this research would have substantial results not only for achieving a better understanding of comparable worth, pay equity, and equal employment opportunity issues, but also for improving our understanding of work and workplaces, wage setting, gender inequality, and social change more generally.

REFERENCES

Beller, Andrea H., and Kee-ok Kim Han
   1984   Occupational sex segregation: Prospects for the 1980s. Pp. 91–114 in Barbara F. Reskin, ed., *Sex Segregation in the Workplace: Trends, Explanations, Remedies*. Committee on Women's Employment and Related Social Issues. Washington, D.C.: National Academy Press.
Bielby, William T., and James N. Baron
   1984a   Men and Women at Work: Gender Segregation Within and Across Organizations. Unpublished paper, University of California, Santa Barbara.
   1984b   A woman's place is with other women: Sex segregation within organizations. Pp. 27–55 in Barbara F. Reskin, ed., *Sex Segregation in the Workplace: Trends, Explanations, Remedies*. Committee on Women's Employment and Related Social Issues. Washington, D.C.: National Academy Press.
Bureau of National Affairs, Inc.
   1984   *Pay Equity and Comparable Worth*. A BNA Special report. Washington, D.C.: Bureau of National Affairs.
Cain, Pamela Stone
   1985   The role of the social sciences in the comparable worth movement. Forthcoming in R. Lance Shotland and Melvin M. Mark, eds., *Social Science and Social Policy*. Beverly Hills, Calif.: Sage Publications.
Collett, Merrill J.
   1983   Comparable worth: An overview. *Public Personnel Management*. Special Issue—Comparable Worth. 12(Winter):325–331.
Cott, Nancy
   1977   *The Bands of Womanhood: "Woman's Sphere" in New England, 1970–1835*. New Haven, Conn.: Yale University Press.

Eisenstein, Sarah
  1983   *Give Us Bread, But Give Us Roses: Working Women's Consciousness in the United States, 1890 to the First World War.* Boston: Routledge & Kegan Paul.
Evans, Mariah D., and Edward O. Laumann
  1983   Professional commitment: Myth or reality? Pp. 3–40 in Donald J. Treiman and Robert V. Robinson, eds., *Research in Social Stratification and Mobility: A Research Annual.* Vol. 2. Greenwich, Conn.: JAI Press.
Gregory, Robert G., and Ronald C. Duncan
  1981   The relevance of segmented labor market theories: The Australian experience of the achievement of equal pay for women. *Journal of Post Keynesian Economics* 3(Spring):403–428.
Hartmann, Heidi I.
  1984   Pay Equity for Women: Wage Discrimination and the Comparable Worth Controversy. Paper presented at the Conference on the Moral Foundations of Civil Rights Policy, University of Maryland, College Park, Md., October 18–20.
Hartmann, Heidi I., and Donald J. Treiman
  1984   Notes on the NAS study of equal pay for jobs of equal value. Ch. 63 in Milton R. Rock, ed., *Handbook of Wage and Salary Administration.* New York: McGraw-Hill.
Jasso, Guillermina, and Peter H. Rossi
  1977   Distributive justice and earned income. *American Sociological Review* 42:639–651.
Kessler-Harris, Alice
  1982   *Out to Work.* New York: Oxford University Press.
Marini, Margaret, and Mary C. Brinton
  1984   Sex-typing in occupational socialization. Pp. 192–232 in Barbara F. Reskin, ed., *Sex Segregation in the Workplace: Trends, Explanations, Remedies.* Committee on Women's Employment and Related Social Issues. Washington, D.C.: National Academy Press.
May, Martha
  1982   The historical problem of the family wage: The Ford Motor Company and the five dollar day. *Feminist Studies* 8(Summer):399–424.
Melosh, Barbara
  1982   *The Physician's Hand.* Philadelphia: Temple University Press. National Committee on Pay Equity, Comparable Worth Project, and the National Women's Political Caucus
National Committee on Pay Equity, Comparable Worth Project, and National Women's Political Caucus
  1984   *Who's Working for Working Women: A Survey of State and Local Government Pay Equity Activities and Initiatives.* Washington, D.C.: Comparable Worth Project, National Committee on Pay Equity, and National Women's Political Caucus.
Norton, Eleanor Holmes
  1979   Speech to Conference on Pay Equity. *Daily Labor Reporter* (BNA), No. 211, October 30.
Ratner, Ronnie Steinberg
  1980   Research: Wage discrimination and pay equity. In Nancy D. Perlman and Bruce J. Ennis, eds., *Preliminary Memorandum on Pay Equity: Achieving Equal Pay for Work of Comparable Value.* Prepared for the Center for Women in Government. Albany, N.Y.: State University of New York.
Reichenberg, Neil E.
  1983   Comparable worth: Recent developments. *Public Personnel Management.* Special Issue—Comparable Worth. 12(Winter):323–324.

Remick, Helen
  1984   Dilemmas of implementation: The case of nursing. Pp. 90–98 in Helen Remick, ed.,
          *Comparable Worth and Wage Discrimination: Technical Possibilities and Political
          Realities.* Philadelphia: Temple University Press.
Remick, Helen, and Ronnie J. Steinberg
  1984   Technical possibilities and political realities: Concluding remarks. Pp. 285–302 in
          Helen Remick, ed., *Comparable Worth and Wage Discrimination: Technical Possibili-
          ties and Political Realities.* Philadelphia: Temple University Press.
Reskin, Barbara F., and Heidi I. Hartmann, eds.
  1985   *Women's Work, Men's Work: Sex Segregation on the Job.* Committee on Women's
          Employment and Related Social Issues. Washington, D.C.: National Academy Press.
Roos, Patricia A.
  1983   Marriage and women's occupational attainment in cross-cultural perspective. *American
          Sociological Review* 48:852–864.
Roos, Patricia A., and Barbara F. Reskin
  1984   Institutional factors contributing to sex segregation in the workplace. Pp. 235–260 in
          Barbara F. Reskin, ed., *Sex Segregation in the Workplace: Trends, Explanations, Reme-
          dies.* Committee on Women's Employment and Related Social Issues. Washington,
          D.C.: National Academy Press.
Treiman, Donald J.
  1977   *Occupational Prestige in Comparative Perspective.* New York: Academic Press.
  1979   *Job Evaluation: An Analytic Review.* Interim Report. Committee on Occupational Clas-
          sification and Analysis. Washington, D.C.: National Academy of Sciences.
  1984a   Effect of choice of factors and factor weights job evaluation. Pp. 79–89 in Helen
          Remick, ed., *Comparable Worth and Wage Discrimination: Technical Possibilities and
          Political Realities.* Philadelphia: Temple University Press.
  1984b   The work histories of women and men: What we know and what we need to find out. Pp.
          213–231 in Alice S. Rossi, ed., *Gender and the Life Course.* New York: Aldine.
Treiman, Donald J., and Heidi I. Hartmann, eds.
  1981   *Women, Work, and Wages: Equal Pay for Jobs of Equal Value.* Final report. Committee
          on Occupational Classification and Analysis. Washington, D.C.: National Academy
          Press.

II
Papers

Job Evaluation Research
and Research Needs

Donald P. Schwab

Job evaluation has been available since the late 1800s and fairly widely implemented by private-sector organizations since the 1930s and especially in the 1940s. Extant research was published largely in the 1940s and 1950s, but it was virtually ignored by investigators in the 1960s and 1970s. Recently, however, spurred largely by interest in comparable worth, attention once again has been focused on job evaluation.

This paper reviews research on job evaluation and suggests appropriate questions and methodologies for the conduct of empirical inquiries needed to assess job evaluation procedures in the context of present challenges. It begins with a brief discussion of perspectives on job evaluation and the implications of these perspectives for the processes central to the installation and maintenance of evaluation systems over time. Existing research investigations bearing on these perspectives and processes are then reviewed as a springboard for suggesting research needed on job evaluation. The discussion of needed research also focuses on issues explicitly evolving from the comparable worth controversy.

PERSPECTIVES

Job evaluation is generally characterized as an administrative procedure designed to help employers develop and maintain job hierarchies for purposes of making pay differentials. Moreover, there is general agreement that the objective of job evaluation is to produce an acceptable pay structure (Munson, 1963:60):

The true function of job evaluation—and it's an important one—is to rationalize and gain acceptability for some way of distributing a batch of money in wages.

Although there is widespread agreement on the general objective of job evaluation, there is considerable disagreement on how acceptability is to be achieved. The dominant perspective views job evaluation from the point of view of applied measurement, with accompanying emphasis on characteristics such as objectivity, generalizability, and parsimony (see, e.g., Viteles, 1941). Industrial psychologists and engineers and most textbook authors have viewed critical job evaluation issues from this point of view.

Acceptability of the results of job evaluation from this perspective is seen as being heavily dependent on the quality of the scores that emerge from the measuring instruments developed to describe and evaluate jobs. To what extent are such scores free from random and systematic errors, for example? How can measuring instruments be changed or improved to reduce such errors?

A very different perspective on job evaluation has emerged from the research and thinking of institutional economists (Kerr and Fisher, 1950; Livernash, 1957). They view job evaluation as a procedure for working out conflicts that inevitably arise about pay differentials over time. These conflicts are largely a function of the fact that internal acceptability (based largely on job content) varies from external acceptability (based largely on market factors). While institutionalists sometimes argue that both internal and external equity are achieved when a job evaluation system is initially installed (e.g., Livernash, 1957), exogenous forces immediately begin to pull them apart. The major task for job evaluation, then, is to accommodate these conflicting forces.

The objectivity of the instrumentation emphasized by the applied measurement perspective contrasts with a view by the institutionalists that sees job evaluation as a flexible set of rules of the game (Kerr and Fisher, 1950:87): "The technical core of a plan (instrumentation), on which so much attention is lavished, has generally less bearing on the ultimate results than either the environment into which it is injected or the policies by which it is administered." Institutionalists, then, emphasize the historical milieu of the system's implementation and the administrative procedures used initially and especially to maintain the system over time. Research and research needs consistent with this orientation thus emphasize the importance of accounting for the context and longitudinal elements of job evaluation processes within organizations.

AVAILABLE RESEARCH

Job evaluation research to date has been most strongly influenced by the applied measurement perspective. Five issues of varying significance have dominated the empirical literature: (1) the reliability of evaluations, (2) the predictability of wage distributions, (3) the convergence between evaluation systems, (4) redundancy in compensable factors, and (5) the impact of rater characteristics on evaluation scores.[1] Each is reviewed briefly below.

1. *Reliability of evaluations.* Of obvious importance to an understanding of job evaluation from a measurement perspective is the question of reliability. More specifically, research has focused on the degree to which evaluations of jobs using point systems are free of random error attributable to the individuals (see, e.g., Ash, 1948; Doverspike et al., 1983; Lawsche and Farbo, 1949; Lawshe and Wilson, 1947) or groups (Schwab and Heneman, 1984) performing the evaluations. In general, studies have found that unreliability is a serious problem in the evaluation of specific compensable factors. Total scores are also unreliably evaluated by single evaluators, although total evaluations from pooled assessments of five or more independently derived judgments tend to be reliable.

As one fairly typical example of this sort of research, Lawshe and Wilson (1947) had 10 raters independently evaluate 20 production jobs on an 11-factor point system. Average correlations between ratings of pairs of evaluators ranged from .34 to .82 for the individual compensable factors, and the average for the total score was r = .77. When the average ratings of 5 of these raters (randomly chosen) were correlated with the pooled ratings of the remaining 5 raters, the resulting correlations among compensable factors ranged from .72 to .96, and the reliability coefficient for the total score was .94. Schwab and Heneman (1984) recently assessed the reliabilities obtained from groups of 3 evaluators using consensus procedures to derive ratings of 53 jobs. The intergroup reliability coefficients resulting from this procedure ranged from .39 to .99 on 10 compensable factors, and the reliability coefficient for the total score was .99.

2. *Predictability of wage distributions.* A large number of demonstrations have been made to show that compensable factor scores (e.g., Chesler, 1948; Davis and Tiffin, 1950; Dertien, 1981; Fitzpatrick, 1947; Fox, 1962; Schwab and Heneman, 1984) and quantitatively derived job analysis scores (e.g., McCormick et al., 1972; Robinson et al., 1974; Tornow and Pinto, 1976) can be weighted (typically using multiple regression) to predict wage distributions with moderate success. By way of illustration, Tornow and Pinto developed a wage prediction model by regressing current wages of 433 managers on 13 evaluation dimensions derived from the Management Position Description Questionnaire. The resulting mathematical model was then used to predict current wages of 56 managers not included in the original

---

[1] See also Schwab (1980b) and Treiman (1979) for review of portions of this research.

sample. The model accounted for 81 percent of the wage variance in the latter group (R = .90).

3. *Convergence between evaluation systems.* Several studies have investigated the extent to which different job evaluation systems yield similar results (Atchison and French, 1967; Chesler, 1948; Dunham, 1978; Robinson et al., 1974; Snelgar, 1983). Table 1 summarizes the results of these studies by showing the lowest and highest degree of convergence (in correlational terms) between different job evaluation systems. As can be seen, results vary widely, with correlation coefficients between systems ranging from a low of .59 (Atchison and French, 1967) to a high of .99 (Snelgar, 1983). Unfortunately, the studies generally do not describe the systems investigated very thoroughly, so it is difficult to understand why there is so much variability in results.

4. *Redundancy in compensable factors.* Point systems often have 10 or more compensable factors on which jobs are evaluated. Using factor analysis or stepwise multiple regression procedures or both, investigators have repeatedly shown that much of the total variance generated by such systems can be explained or accounted for by just a few factors or dimensions (e.g., Davis and Tiffin, 1950; Grant, 1951; Howard and Schutz, 1952; Lawshe, 1945; Lawshe and Maleski, 1946; Lawshe et al., 1948). As one example, Lawshe et al. (1948) found that just 3 compensable factors were necessary to account for from 86 to 96 percent of the variance in the total scores generated from a system of 11 compensable factors used in three firms. This sort of finding is obtained because compensable factors in point systems tend to be highly intercorrelated (colinear).

5. *Impact of rater characteristics on evaluation scores.* Finally, there have been investigations of whether traits or situational characteristics of evaluators influence mean ratings or reliability. Although there is some

TABLE 1   Convergence of Results Across Alternative Job Evaluation Systems

Study	No. of Plans	Range of Correlation Coefficients	
		Low	High
Atchison and French (1967)	3	.54	.82
Chesler (1948)	3[a]	.85	.97
Dunham (1978)	6	.89	.97
Robinson et al. (1974)	5[a]	.82	.95
Snelgar (1983)[b]	16	.77	.99

[a] Includes Market Wage Survey as a "system."

[b] Includes a sample of "heterogeneous" and a sample of "homogeneous" jobs.

evidence that evaluators' familiarity with jobs influences mean ratings (Madden, 1962, 1963), research does not suggest that evaluations by managers differ appreciably from those by incumbents (Chambliss, 1950) or union representatives (Lawshe and Farbo, 1949). Of more direct relevance to the comparable worth controversy, a few studies have found that evaluations (Doverspike et al., 1983; Schwab and Grams, in press) or quantitative job analysis scores (Arvey et al., 1977) do not differ as a function of the sex of the evaluator.

RESEARCH AGENDA

The paucity of research on job evaluation reviewed here may come as a surprise, given the significance of job evaluation to compensation administration. Clearly, there are a large number of relevant research issues even without the challenges of comparable worth. Questions raised by advocates and critics of comparable worth simply compound that number. What follows is an attempt to suggest important questions that require research answers, especially if job evaluation is to be considered as a mechanism for achieving comparable worth (however defined). It begins with issues that have been raised specifically in a comparable worth context, issues that follow closely from the applied measurement perspective. These are followed by a set of broader, more descriptive questions, which reflect to a greater degree the institutionalist perspective.

Issues Stimulated by Comparable Worth

While advocates of comparable worth have raised many specific criticisms of current job evaluation, their major concerns fall within two broad categories. The first and most important concern has to do with the criterion used to weight compensable factor scores. The second has to do with biases that may occur in the evaluation process itself. Each of these as well as potentially useful research to be performed is discussed below.

The Criterion

As currently used in the private sector, job evaluation is typically validated against a wage criterion (e.g., Schwab, 1980b; Treiman and Hartmann, 1981). That is, the acceptability of job evaluation results are initially determined by the correspondence between the job hierarchy produced by the evaluation system and some existing distribution of wages for those jobs. Sometimes this is done via "policy capturing," wherein the compensable factors are formally weighted to maximize the relationship between evaluation results and wages (Treiman, 1979). In all probability the process is more often done less formally, but, in any event, correspondence between evaluation results and current wages is an important element in determining the acceptability of the system to the employer.

Advocates of comparable worth have, of course, raised objections to the use of wages as the criterion, because they conclude that existing wage distributions are biased against jobs held mainly by women (e.g., Blumrosen, 1979; Treiman and Hartmann, 1981). If wages are biased, and if wages serve as the criterion for job evaluation, that bias will be reflected in the job evaluation results (Schwab and Wichern, 1983).[2]

As a consequence, some analysts have suggested that wages not be used as the criterion or, if used, "corrected" for sex bias (e.g., Blumrosen, 1979; Treiman and Hartmann, 1981). Although these recommendations are far from universally accepted (see, e.g., McCormick, 1981; Milkovich, 1980; Milkovich and Broderick, 1982; Nelson et al., 1980), empirical research and theory addressing the criterion question are clearly appropriate. What are alternatives to using wages for weighting compensable factors, and what are the implications of such alternatives?

A not inconsequential advantage of an observable criterion such as a wage distribution stems from the fact that it simplifies and makes "objective" the weighting of compensable factors. Once the criterion is agreed on, the procedure for weighting and for determining how well the resulting model "fits" the criterion distribution can proceed statistically. Job evaluation implemented in this manner represents a form of criterion-related (empirical) validation. Alternatively, specification of an unobservable conceptual criterion such as worth casts the problem into the domain of construct validation (Schwab, 1980b). Not only is establishing construct validity more difficult, but also the standards for deciding when adequate validity has been achieved are less amenable to unambiguous interpretation and hence agreement (see, e.g., Schwab, 1980a).

It would appear highly desirable, therefore, if observable criteria could be generated against which job evaluation instruments could be developed and validated. Unfortunately, comparable worth advocates generally have not made suggestions regarding alternative observable criteria. What follows is thus highly tentative; it is only a suggestion for how research investigating observable criteria for job evaluation might proceed.

A starting point might be to focus on the objective of job evaluation, a conceptual criterion that commentators agree on, namely, acceptability of

---

[2] An obvious question pertains to the veracity of the comparable worth conclusion. Are market wages biased against jobs held mainly by women? Issues pertaining to this question are not considered in the present paper.

the outcomes to the participants (see also Munson, 1963, on this issue). Could participants agree, for example, on compensable factors and weights that produced perceptually equitable job hierarchies?

The existing job evaluation literature will probably be of little help in identifying likely compensable factors for such a criterion. There seems to be general agreement that existing job evaluation plans have emerged without much thought or research (e.g., Belcher, 1974; Nash and Carroll, 1975). In the historical evolution of the procedure, compensable factors were found that "predicted" market wages; little further development took place, since the major organizational objective was easily achieved.

Equity theory (e.g., Adams, 1963) may be of greater value for identifying compensable factors that will produce perceptually equitable job distributions. Although most research in an employment context has focused on behavioral consequences of inequity (for a review see, e.g., Campbell and Pritchard, 1976), a growing body of literature has examined equity determinants, particularly in a compensation context (e.g., Belcher and Atchison, 1970; Birnbaum, 1983; Dyer et al., 1976; Goodman, 1975; Lawler, 1966). Although these studies have emphasized individual rather than job characteristics, they nevertheless may serve as methodological models for job-evaluation-oriented investigations.

One model appears especially well suited to the problem at hand. Specifically, once compensable factors have been tentatively identified, policy capturing (see, e.g., Slovic and Lichtenstein, 1971) could be employed to specify weights and to ascertain the degree of agreement within and between representative samples of management and employee groups.

If this line of inquiry appears fruitful (i.e., if compensable factors can be found and weighted to predict perceptually equitable job hierarchies), subsequent research can compare results with those obtained from more traditional job evaluation methods and with existing wage distributions. Judgments could then be made about whether the results would be acceptable in terms of political and economic considerations.

Evaluation Bias

The second general concern expressed is the possibility that job evaluation is developed or implemented so that the resulting job hierarchies lead to wage underpayment for predominantly female jobs. "It is likely that most, if not all, job-evaluation systems contain sex bias" (Collette, 1982:154). Such bias could be manifested in several ways.

One potential difficulty discussed has to do with the compensable factors included in the job evaluation system. It has been frequently hypothesized that compensable factors in conventional job evaluation plans favor work done in predominantly male jobs (e.g., Blumrosen, 1979; Grune, 1982; Remick, 1981; Thomsen, 1977; Treiman, 1979). Evidence supportive of this hypothesis, however, is scarce. Indeed, it is difficult to envision a methodology that would test this hypothesis unambiguously.

For example, Doverspike and Barrett (1984) compared sets of predominantly female with predominantly male jobs on 15 compensable factors. They then took as evidence of bias any difference between the male and female job sets on a number of psychometric characteristics (e.g., reliability, mean differences, and so forth). However, to assume that bias in this instance means anything other than difference, one must additionally assume that (a) ratings were not a function of raters (i.e., no rater bias), and (b) the two job sets were psychometrically identical in some "true" score sense. Given the degree of occupational sex-related segregation known to exist, the latter assumption is particularly hard to accept. Consequently, it is difficult to conclude from such an exercise that anything very meaningful has been learned about potential bias in compensable factors.

A second hypothesis about an error source that could be to the wage disadvantage of predominantly female jobs has to do with bias in either the description or the evaluation of jobs. Analysts or evaluators may deliberately or inadvertently denigrate jobs performed predominantly by women (Grune, 1982; Remick, 1981; Schwab, 1980b; Thomsen, 1981; Treiman, 1979; Treiman and Hartmann, 1981).

This hypothesis has been addressed from two perspectives. As already noted in this review, several studies found little evidence that judgments of jobs vary as a function of the sex of the evaluator. If sex stereotypes about jobs exist, they apparently transcend the sex of the individual making the judgment. Several studies have also been performed that have tried to directly identify sex stereotypes. Arvey et al. (1977) investigated bias in job analysis by having subjects evaluate two jobs identical in all respects except that one was characterized as female, the other as male (manipulated with photographs). They found no differences as a function of the sex characterization of the job. Three studies have addressed sex bias in the evaluation of jobs. In a correlational study Mahoney and Blake (1979) found that the perceived femininity of an occupation explained a small but statistically significant amount of recommended salary variance after controlling for effects due to job characteristics. Experimental studies alternatively have found little evidence that student evaluators were influenced by the sex composition of a set of jobs (Grams and Schwab, 1985) and no evidence that experienced compensation specialists or administrators were so influenced (Schwab and Grams, in press).

Thus, the evidence to date does not provide much support for the hypothesis that the sex of the job per se influences job descriptions or evaluations. This evidence, however, is limited, and there is an obvious need for additional research. It is especially important that these sorts of investigations study alternative types of job analysis and evaluation instruments and that they manipulate job stereotypes in alternative ways.

A potential source of bias that has not been previously considered in the comparable worth debate did obtain support in both the Grams and Schwab (1985) and Schwab and Grams (in press) experiments. Specifically, both studies found evidence that evaluations were substantially influenced by the current salary reported for the jobs studied. While more research is again called for, the implications of this finding for wage fairness are potentially profound. For if there is sex bias in current wage structures, replicated evidence that wage rates influence evaluations suggests that bias could enter evaluation results even though salaries are not used as an explicit external criterion in validating the system.

Contextual Issues

The research questions posed above are understandably narrow in the sense that they focus on differential job evaluation results as a function of the predominant sex of the job incumbents. They are also narrow, it seems to me, in the assumptions they make about the job evaluation process as it is conducted in organizations. The issues identified below are illustrative of contextual and more basic information needed to thoroughly understand how job evaluation is used by organizations and how it affects resulting wage structures.

Despite the presumption that job evaluation is widely used by organizations and that its use is increasing (e.g., Nash and Carroll, 1975), few reliable data exist on the number of firms using it, the types of systems used, the jobs included, or the employees covered. Descriptive information on such questions tends to come from ad hoc surveys that have been conducted only periodically. Inferences about general usage have often been drawn from samples of unknown populations.

As a result, a reasonable foundation for a systematic investigation of job evaluation might well begin with comprehensive descriptive data on its use, especially in the private sector. Such a survey should go beyond merely documenting types of plans (point system versus classification, and so forth) and obtain information on the specific procedures used to evaluate and price jobs.

Evaluation Processes

An illustration may be helpful in suggesting the type of information that I believe is needed about how job evaluation is conducted and the importance of obtaining such information for subsequent research. Investigations to date have tended to use similar methodologies to study job evaluation. The studies described above have nearly always had evaluators independently examine one or more written job descriptions and then evaluate those descriptions using some variant of a common point system. To what extent does this procedure describe organizational practice?

My experience with organizations implementing job evaluation is that the evaluators frequently begin by generating the job descriptions and that, in the process, they obtain information from incumbents, supervisors, and other sources. Schwab and Grams (1983) provide a somewhat more representative confirmation that evaluators typically have substantially more information than is provided by written descriptions when making judgments about jobs. Whether these data increase evaluation accuracy or merely add error variance is largely unknown at this point, but certainly their presence raises questions about the external validity of the research that has been performed.

Pricing Jobs

Descriptive information is also needed about the mechanisms that organizations use to price job hierarchies following the initial evaluation process. Treiman (1979) reported that it is customary for organizations to weight compensable factors so that the relationship with some wage distribution is maximized. To what extent does this actually apply? What procedures are used to maximize the relationship (reevaluation of jobs, changes in the evaluation instrumentation, elimination of outlier jobs, and so forth)? What criteria, if any, are used when wages are not employed in this fashion? Inferences about what job evaluation accomplishes will not be very informed until we have more data on how organizations use it to make compensation decisions.

It is especially important to obtain information about pricing decisions following initial implementation. Regardless of how the job hierarchy is priced when the system is first installed, what happens to wage structures over time and what adjustments in other personnel or human resources systems are made to accommodate the job evaluation system? Livernash (1957) noted that pressures emerge on the job evaluation system as changes occur either in the external wage contours of the organization (e.g., changes in differential labor demand patterns, modifications in union relationships) or in internal job content (e.g., as a function of product or technological change).

On the basis of field observations, Slichter et al. (1960) and Kerr and Fisher (1950) reported that job evaluation systems can easily fail unless administrative procedures and practices account for these changes. Kerr and

Fisher in particular suggest not only that alterations are made in the wage structures emerging from job evaluation, but also that other personnel or human resource systems are modified to accommodate wage structure pressures. In the air manufacturing industry, for example, they observed not only job reevaluation, inflation of job descriptions, and demoralization of the merit pay systems but also changes in training programs, recruiting practices, and job redesign. Personal conversations with compensation administrators suggest that these responses are far from unique.

If organizations routinely modify wage structures following implementation,[3] problems are necessarily increased for those who wish to achieve any sort of specific objective through job evaluation (e.g., a homogeneous standard of internal equity). The research of the institutionalists suggests that in order to respond to the multiple and potentially conflicting claims of equity, job evaluation systems must remain flexible (i.e., to some extent they must tolerate distortion). Clearly, current and more representative evidence is needed regarding this important possibility.

SUMMARY AND CONCLUSIONS

Job evaluation has been thought about and studied from two perspectives. One of these, emphasizing the importance of applied measurement, views job evaluation largely as a scaling system for generating "true" job scores on compensable factors. The other perspective, the institutional view, emphasizes the role of the job evaluation system in dealing with the conflicts that occur between internal (organizational) and external (market) forces and values.

Research on job evaluation has been dominated by the applied measurement perspective. Thus a good bit of research has been conducted on the quality of the scores emerging from the evaluation of jobs on compensable factors. In particular, research has been performed on the reliability of scores, the validity of those scores for predicting current wage differentials, convergence between alternative evaluation systems and between compensable factors, and the degree to which scores are a function of the individuals performing the evaluations.

Research questions suggested by the comparable worth controversy so far have fallen largely within the purview of the applied measurement perspec-

---

[3] Indeed, Kerr and Fisher (1950) argued that such modifications are necessary if the job evaluation system is to remain viable. "The more fixed, definite, and self executing the formula [the formal job evaluation plan], the less will it allow for the other and perhaps more important pressures to which wage rates respond" (p. 94).

tive. Questions have been raised especially about the quality of the criterion used to weight compensable factor scores and about the possibility that such scores are biased in various ways to the disadvantage of jobs held largely by women.

These are certainly appropriate questions, and a number of suggestions for how such research might proceed are offered in this paper. Nevertheless, it seems to me that the more fundamental challenge to an understanding of job evaluation rests in the institutional perspective. Job evaluation is a complex system, complexly related to a number of other personnel systems (e.g., wage surveys) in the organization. A great number of judgments are necessary to set up such systems and to maintain them over time. Until we learn much more about how these judgments are made, about their consequences, and about the exogenous factors that influence them, we run the risk of establishing policies that will not accomplish the objectives sought.

A number of the research questions suggested in this paper fall within the institutional domain. These, it seems to me, are more basic than the applied measurement issues that have so far dominated the comparable worth debate. However, no claim is made that the institutional issues raised here are exhaustive, or that they are even the most critical to our understanding of job evaluation processes. So bereft are we of views of job evaluation from an institutional perspective that further work needs to be performed just to specify a reasonable research agenda.

ACKNOWLEDGMENT

Financial assistance from the Graduate School of Business and the Graduate School, University of Wisconsin-Madison, is gratefully acknowledged. Helpful comments on an earlier draft were made by Chris Berger, Bob Grams, Heidi Hartmann, and Tom Mahoney.

REFERENCES

Adams, J.S.
   1963   Toward an understanding of inequity. *Journal of Abnormal and Social Psychology* 67:422–436.
Arvey, R.D., E.M. Passino, and J.W. Lounsbury
   1977   Job analysis results as influenced by sex of incumbent and sex of analyst. *Journal of Applied Psychology* 62:411–416.
Ash, P.
   1948   The reliability of job evaluation rankings. *Journal of Applied Psychology* 32:313–320.
Atchison, T., and W. French
   1967   Pay systems for scientists and engineers. *Industrial Relations* 7:44-56.
Belcher, D.W.
   1974   *Compensation Administration*. Englewood Cliffs, N.J.: Prentice-Hall.

Belcher, D.W., and T.J. Atchison
1970   Equity theory and compensation policy. *Personnel Administration* 33(3):22-33.
Birnbaum, M.H.
1983   Perceived equity of salary policies. *Journal of Applied Psychology* 68(1):49-59.
Blumrosen, R.G.
1979   Wage discrimination, job segregation, and Title VII of the Civil Rights Act of 1964. *University of Michigan Journal of Law Reform* 12:397-502.
Campbell, J.P., and R.D. Pritchard
1976   Motivation theory in industrial and organizational psychology. Pp. 63-130 in M.D. Dunnette, ed., *Handbook of Industrial and Organizational Psychology*. Chicago: Rand McNally.
Chambliss, L.A.
1950   Our employees evaluate their own jobs. *Personnel Journal* 29(4):141-142.
Chesler, D.J.
1948   Reliability and comparability of different job evaluation systems. *Journal of Applied Psychology* 32:465-475.
Collette, C.O.
1982   Ending sex discrimination in wage setting. Pp. 150-155 in *Proceedings of the 35th Annual Meeting of the Industrial Relations Research Association*. Madison, Wis.: Industrial Relations Research Association.
Davis, M.K., and J. Tiffin
1950   Cross validation of an abbreviated point job evaluation system. *Journal of Applied Psychology* 34:225-228.
Dertien, M.G.
1981   The accuracy of job evaluation plans. *Personnel Journal* 60:566-570.
Doverspike, D., and G.V. Barrett
1984   An internal bias analysis of a job evaluation instrument. *Journal of Applied Psychology* 69:648-662.
Doverspike, D., A.M. Carlisi, G.V. Barrett, and R.A. Alexander
1983   Generalizability analysis of a point-method job evaluation instrument. *Journal of Applied Psychology* 68:476-483.
Dunham, R.B.
1978   Job Evaluation: Two Instruments on Sources of Pay Satisfaction. Paper presented at the American Psychological Association, Toronto.
Dyer, L., D.P. Schwab, and R.D. Theriault
1976   Managerial perceptions regarding salary increase criteria. *Personnel Psychology* 29:233-242.
Fitzpatrick, B.H.
1947   An objective test of job evaluation validity. *Personnel Journal* 28(9):128-132.
Fox, W.M.
1962   Purpose and validity in job evaluation. *Personnel Journal* 41:332-337.
Goodman, P.S.
1975   Effect of perceived inequity on salary allocation decisions. *Journal of Applied Psychology* 60(3):372-375.
Grams, R., and D.P. Schwab
1985   Systematic sex-related error in job evaluation. *Academy of Management Journal*. (Forthcoming)
Grant, D.L.
1951   An analysis of a point rating job evaluation plan. *Journal of Applied Psychology* 35:236-240.

Grune, J.A.
1982   Comparable worth: Issues and perspectives. Discussion. Pp. 169–172 in *Proceedings of the 35th Annual Meeting of the Industrial Relations Research Association*. Madison, Wis.: Industrial Relations Research Association.

Howard, A.H., and H.G. Schutz
1952   A factor analysis of a salary job evaluation plan. *Journal of Applied Psychology* 36:243–246.

Kerr, C., and L.H. Fisher
1950   Effect of environment and administration on job evaluation. *Harvard Business Review* 28(3):77–96.

Lawler, E.E., III
1966   Managers' attitudes toward how their pay is and should be determined. *Journal of Applied Psychology* 50:273–279.

Lawshe, C.H., Jr.
1945   Studies in job evaluation: II. The adequacy of abbreviated point ratings for hourly-paid jobs in three industrial plants. *Journal of Applied Psychology* 29:177–184.

Lawshe, C.H., Jr., and P.C. Farbo
1949   Studies in job evaluation: 8. The reliability of an abbreviated job evaluation system. *Journal of Applied Psychology* 33:158–166.

Lawshe, C.H., Jr., and A.A. Maleski
1946   Studies in job evaluation: 3. An analysis of point ratings for salary paid jobs in an industrial plant. *Journal of Applied Psychology* 30:117–128.

Lawshe, C.H., Jr., and R.F. Wilson
1947   Studies in job evaluation: 6. The reliability of two point rating systems. *Journal of Applied Psychology* 31:355–365.

Lawshe, C.H., Jr., E.E. Dudek, and R.F. Wilson
1948   Studies in job evaluation: 7. A factor analysis of two point rating methods of job evaluation. *Journal of Applied Psychology* 32:118–129.

Livernash, E.R.
1957   The internal wage structure. Pp. 140–172 in G.W. Taylor and F.C. Pierson, eds., *New Concepts in Wage Determination*. New York: McGraw-Hill.

Madden, J.M.
1962   The effect of varying the degree of rater familiarity in job evaluation. *Personnel Administrator* 25:42–46.

1963   A further note on the familiarity effect in job evaluation. *Personnel Administration* 26:52–53.

Mahoney, T.A., and R.H. Blake
1979   Occupational Pay as a Function of Sex Stereotypes and Job Content. Paper presented at the meeting of the National Academy of Management, Atlanta.

McCormick, E.J.
1981   Minority report. Pp. 115–130 in D.J. Treiman and H.I. Hartmann, eds., *Women, Work, and Wages: Equal Pay for Jobs of Equal Value*. Committee on Occupational Classification and Analysis. Washington, D.C.: National Academy Press.

McCormick, E.J., P.R. Jeanneret, and R.C. Mecham
1972   A study of job characteristics and job dimensions as based on the Position Analysis Questionnaire (PAQ). *Journal of Applied Psychology* 56:347–368.

Milkovich, G.T.
1980   The emerging debate. Pp. 23–47 in E.R. Livernash, ed., *Comparable Worth: Issues and Alternatives*. Washington, D.C.: Equal Employment Advisory Council.

Milkovich, G.T., and R. Broderick
  1982   Pay discrimination: Legal issues and implications for research. *Industrial Relations* 21:309–317.
Munson, F.
  1963   Four fallacies for wage and salary administrators. *Personnel* 40(4):57–64.
Nash, A.N., and S.J. Carroll, Jr.
  1975   *The Management of Compensation.* Monterey, Calif.: Brooks/Cole.
Nelson, B.A., E.M. Opton, Jr., and T.E. Wilson
  1980   Wage discrimination and the "comparable worth" theory in perspective. *University of Michigan Journal of Law Reform* 13:231–301.
Remick, H.
  1981   The comparable worth controversy. *Public Personnel Management* 10:371–383.
Robinson, D.D., O.W. Wahlstrom, and R.C. Mecham
  1974   Comparison of job evaluation methods: A "policy-capturing" approach using the Position Analysis Questionnaire (PAQ). *Journal of Applied Psychology* 59:633–637.
Schwab, D.P.
  1980a   Construct validity in organizational behavior. Pp. 3–43 in B. Staw and L.L. Cummings, eds., *Research in Organizational Behavior.* Vol. 2. Greenwich, Conn.: JAI Press.
  1980b   Job evaluation and pay setting: Concepts and practices. Pp. 49–77 in E.R. Livernash, ed., *Comparable Worth: Issues and Alternatives.* Washington, D.C.: Equal Employment Advisory Council.
Schwab, D.P., and R. Grams
  1983   A Survey of Job Evaluation Practice Among Compensation Specialists: A Summary of Findings. Technical Report, American Compensation Association, Scottsdale, Ariz.
  In   Sex-related errors in job evaluation: A "real-world" test. *Journal of Applied Psychol-*
  press   *ogy.*
Schwab, D.P., and H.G. Heneman, III
  1984   Assessment of a Consensus-Based Multiple Information Source Job Evaluation System. Paper presented at the National Academy of Management Meetings, Boston.
Schwab, D.P., and D.W. Wichern
  1983   Systematic bias in job evaluation and market wages: Implications for the comparable worth debate. *Journal of Applied Psychology* 31:353–364.
Slichter, S.H., J.J. Healy, and E.R. Livernash
  1960   *The Impact of Collective Bargaining on Management.* Washington, D.C.: Brookings Institution.
Slovic, P., and S. Lichtenstein
  1971   Comparison of Bayesian and regression approaches to the study of information processing in judgment. *Organizational Behavior and Human Performance* 6:649–744.
Snelgar, R.J.
  1983   The comparability of job evaluation methods in supplying approximately similar classifications in rating one job series. *Personnel Psychology* 36:371–380.
Thomsen, D.J.
  1977   Unmentioned problems of salary administration. *American Compensation Review* (4):11–21.
  1981   Compensation and benefits: More on comparable worth. *Personnel Journal* 60:348–354.
Tornow, W.W., and P.R. Pinto
  1976   The development of a managerial job taxonomy: A system for describing, classifying, and evaluating executive positions. *Journal of Applied Psychology* 61:410–418.

Treiman, D.J.
  1979   *Job Evaluation: An Analytical Review*. Interim Report to the Equal Employment Oppor-
         tunity Commission. Committee on Occupational Classification and Analysis. Washing-
         ton, D.C.: National Academy of Sciences.
Treiman, D.J., and H.I. Hartmann, eds.
  1981   *Women, Work, and Wages: Equal Pay for Jobs of Equal Value*. Committee on Occupa-
         tional Classification and Analysis. Washington, D.C.: National Academy Press.
Viteles, M.S.
  1941   A psychologist looks at job evaluation. *Personnel* 17(3):165–176.

Social Judgment Biases
in Comparable Worth Analysis

Leslie Zebrowitz McArthur

The pros and cons of a policy of remunerating jobs according to their comparable worth have been hotly debated in recent months. Most of the arguments in this debate have been economic ones. An issue that has received less attention, but that is equally problematic, is the difficulty of generating accurate job evaluations. Determining the comparable worth of jobs involves three major judgmental tasks: (1) to choose the set of compensable factors that contribute to the value of jobs as well as the weight that should be accorded to each factor, (2) to describe the jobs, and (3) to evaluate how much of each compensable factor is contained in each job. Because these tasks are difficult and inherently subjective, they can overtax people's ability to render accurate, unbiased judgments. In particular, considerable research has established that when people are faced with a complex inferential task, such as comparable worth assessment, their judgments are vulnerable to a number of biases resulting from unequal attention to the various elements of information provided. Such selective attention can favor information that is most readily recalled, an "availability bias." It can also favor evaluatively consistent information, a "halo bias." And it can favor information that is congruent with existing beliefs, an "expectancy bias." It is important to note that these biases do not necessarily indicate any desire to distort the information provided; rather, it is people's cognitive limitations that produce biased judgments. The purpose of this paper is to discuss evidence documenting social judgment biases as it pertains to comparable worth analyses and to suggest research that could elucidate the least-biased procedures for establishing the comparable worth of jobs.

53

CHOOSING AN INSTRUMENT FOR JOB DESCRIPTION

In choosing a job description instrument for comparable worth analyses of men's and women's jobs, the goal is to select one that (1) provides job descriptions that are not biased in favor of either men's jobs or women's jobs, (2) differentiates equally well among women's jobs and men's jobs, and (3) measures all job elements that are deemed pertinent to wages. Although considerable research will be necessary to determine whether these conditions are met by any of the existing job description procedures, it is clear that certain methods are much more vulnerable to bias than others. On one hand there are qualitative, narrative descriptions of jobs. Unconstrained by particular rating dimensions, such descriptions are likely to be heavily influenced by biases resulting from unequal attention to various aspects of the information provided. Structured job descriptions, on the other hand, are likely to minimize bias that results from a failure to even think about job elements that are not already salient. Such descriptions have the further advantage of allowing one to quantitatively compare a variety of different jobs on a set of common dimensions. In addition, they permit one to assess the consensual validity of job descriptions by comparing those provided by a variety of sources, something that is less feasible with narrative descriptions, which cannot readily be provided by incumbents, supervisors, and outside experts alike.

Despite their advantages, structured job descriptions are not without problems. All the biases discussed in this paper may enter into job descriptions even when they are provided through ratings on a set of structured dimensions. Another problem is that existing measures may be more applicable to some jobs than to others. For example, one structured job analysis measure, the Position Analysis Questionnaire (PAQ) (McCormick et al., 1969) has been reported to be better at differentiating among manual occupations, which are typically held by men, than among clerical ones, which are typically held by women (Frieling, 1977). To be useful for purposes of establishing comparable worth, a structured job analysis must be equally applicable to a wide variety of jobs.

The development of a structured instrument that provides descriptions of men's and women's jobs that are not obviously sex-biased and that differentiates equally well among various occupations is a necessary but not sufficient condition for establishing the comparable worth of jobs. One must also establish the validity of the instrument for measuring job elements that are deemed pertinent to wages. An instrument that is useful for personnel selection—e.g., determining the kinds of abilities that are needed for a particular job—may or may not be useful for setting wages. However, at least one instrument does have proven validity in measuring job elements that are relevant to both. The Position Analysis Questionnaire has been shown to predict not only aptitude requirements for a wide variety of jobs but also their going rates of pay (McCormick et al., 1972).

Some advocates of the structured job analysis procedure argue that the ability of an instrument like the PAQ to predict existing wages renders it sufficient to determine job worth. In particular, they argue that one should employ statistical procedures to determine what elements of job descriptions predict existing wages and from these data determine the worth of various jobs (e.g., McCormick et al., 1972). Others (e.g., Treiman and Hartmann, 1981), however, have aptly pointed out that this "policy capturing" approach yields comparable worth scores for jobs that perpetuate any inequities in existing wages. For this reason, although structured job analysis procedures may be useful for describing jobs, evaluating the comparable worth of jobs requires determining which job elements should be compensated, rather than relying on market indicators of which job elements are currently compensated. Given that this is the ultimate goal of the job description, it might make more sense to begin by defining the compensable factors and then generating a descriptive instrument that has been specifically designed to describe job elements that are likely to be related to the compensable factors. Such an approach could aid in difficult decisions regarding the content of the job descriptions, such as how much coverage should be given to job elements (what the worker does), worker attributes (skills, training), and the job environment.

POTENTIAL BIASES IN JOB DESCRIPTIONS AND EVALUATIONS

The Availability Bias

The availability heuristic (Tversky and Kahneman, 1974) is the tendency of people to assess the frequency or probability of events by the ease with which instances or occurrences can be brought to mind. In the realm of job descriptions it would be manifested in a tendency to describe the frequency of certain job-related activities according to their ease of retrieval from memory. However, ease of retrieval may not bear a one-to-one relationship to the actual frequency of the activity. Rather, it may be influenced by variables such as the familiarity of the activity, its recency, or its perceptual salience.

One example of bias resulting from the availability heuristic is provided in research that has demonstrated that people tend to overestimate their own contribution to products and outcomes that are produced jointly with others (Ross, 1981). This tendency seems to be produced by the greater availability in memory of one's own efforts. Such a bias in job analysis could cause incumbents to overestimate their own job's contribution to various endeavors. Similarly, it could cause supervisors to underestimate the contributions made by the jobs of their subordinates insofar as their own contributions are more available in memory. In addition to the potential of the availability heuristic to produce this general egocentric bias in job descriptions, it could have more specific effects. For example, secretarial job descriptions provided by supervisors might overestimate the job element of typing because this noisy activity is more perceptually salient than is the quieter activity of composing literate and tactful letters. Similarly, job descriptions for physicians might overestimate the job element of examining patients because this is a more familiar and hence more available element of the job than is bookkeeping, which may be underestimated.

Generally speaking, the operation of the availability heuristic could produce different job descriptions by incumbents, supervisors, and outside experts. More specifically, outside experts may overestimate the frequency of those activities that are the most familiar to them; incumbents may overestimate the frequency of those activities that they have performed most recently; and supervisors may overestimate the frequency of those activities that are the most perceptually salient—i.e., those activities that supervisors can see or hear. The potential influence of the availability heuristic suggests that in implementing any job evaluation procedure, one very important decision to make is who will describe the jobs.

There are certain advantages to using job descriptions prepared by incumbents. For one thing, incumbents have the potential to provide the best-informed description of the job tasks and the working environment, since they are the most intimately involved with the jobs. Incumbents' job descriptions should also be less costly to obtain than descriptions from outside experts. In addition, one might expect that incumbents' job descriptions would be the most satisfactory to employees involved in litigation to raise their wages. Of course, the acceptability of these descriptions to employers must also be ensured. More specifically, it must be demonstrated that job descriptions by incumbents are reliable and valid. Unfortunately, this is not an easy task.

There is some evidence for the reliability of incumbents' job descriptions. For example, a longitudinal study found that individuals' perceptions of task characteristics were relatively stable over a 3-month period (Griffen, 1981). In addition to evidence for the reliability of job descriptions across time, there is also evidence for inter-rater reliability (e.g., Desmond and Weiss, 1973, 1975; Fischer and Sobkow, 1979). More specifically, when incumbents from a wide variety of occupations provided questionnaire ratings of the degree of various abilities that their own jobs required, the results revealed high inter-rater agreement among workers in a given job regarding the requisite abilities. Moreover, there was more agreement in the ratings of workers on the job than among workers in general. It thus appears that incumbents can provide reliable information about the ability requirements of their own jobs.

Establishing the validity of incumbents' job descriptions is a more difficult task than establishing their reliability. However, there is some evidence regarding convergent validity. Generally speaking, the ability requirements described by incumbents, supervisors, and experts in the foregoing research were all very similar to one another, but there were some discrepancies—that is, incumbents would rate a particular ability as very important for job performance, while experts would not, or vice versa. Discrepancies in the job descriptions provided by different sources have been found for job elements other than requisite abilities. In particular, researchers found differences in perceptions of the work climate by workers and employers (Narayanan and Venkatachalam, 1982). Further research is needed to determine whether there is convergent validity in various sources' descriptions of still other job elements, such as the responsibility or the effort that a job entails. Job descriptions on these dimensions seem more vulnerable to the availability bias, and it is possible that incumbents will show less agreement with supervisors or experts than they do when describing requisite abilities.

It should be noted that the availability bias can affect evaluations of job worth on various compensable factors just as it can affect job descriptions. If an analyst reads an entire job description and then makes ratings of job worth on a number of dimensions, these ratings may be overly influenced by the descriptive elements that are most available in memory. Moreover, if the jobs have been labeled or are otherwise identifiable, the descriptive elements that are most available in memory may well be those that are most familiar by virtue of preconceptions about the jobs. If so, the resulting evaluations of worth will be biased toward the status quo. One way to deal with this problem is to have each element in the job description rated separately as to its worth on the set of compensable factors. Another is to have this task performed by a computer programmed to allocate some predetermined "worth" or "job points" for each element in the job description.

The Halo Bias

Considerable research has demonstrated that most social judgments tend to be evaluatively consistent. Thus, for example, people who are labeled as "good" on some important dimension are surrounded with a positive aura, or "halo," which causes other positive qualities to be ascribed to them.

Conversely, people who are labeled as "bad" on some important dimension are perceived as having a number of other negative qualities—the "negative halo" or "forked tail" effect (e.g., Kelley, 1950).

The operation of halo biases in social judgments may have important implications for comparable worth analyses. In particular, job descriptions and evaluations of worth may be strongly influenced by a job's prestige or its assumed salary. In keeping with this suggestion, Grams and Schwab (1985) found that when a job was presented as having low pay, it was evaluated as less worthy on a series of compensable factors than the same job presented as having higher pay. The power of the halo bias in assessments of job worth was even more strikingly revealed in the results of a study by McArthur and Obrant (1984). These authors found that analysts' judgments about the traditional compensable factors of skill and responsibility did not predict their evaluations of a job's monetary worth, while their judgments about the job's salary and its desirability (ignoring salary) were strongly predictive of rated worth. A third variable that independently predicted ratings of the job's monetary worth was the gender of the incumbent: female incumbents were associated with lower worth. Since it has been found that rising numbers of female incumbents may lower the prestige of an occupation while rising numbers of male incumbents may raise occupational prestige (Touhey, 1974a, 1974b), this result can also be interpreted as a halo bias.

The tendency for a woman incumbent to depress judgments of a job's monetary worth suggests that a halo deriving from the sex composition of a job may also bias job analysis. More specifically, occupations that are dominated by men may be evaluated more favorably than those that are dominated by women. However, Grams and Schwab (1985) found that the manipulated percentage of women in a job had no consistent impact on evaluations of the job on three compensable factors: education required, experience required, and job complexity. Similarly, whereas the gender of the incumbent had strong effects on job descriptions and evaluations of worth in the research of McArthur and Obrant (1984), the manipulated sex composition of workers in the occupation had no significant effects at all.[1] While these findings do not reveal the predicted halo bias, they are actually consistent with another social judgment bias—the "vividness bias." That is, it has been found that people's social judgments are relatively insensitive to abstract information concerning population "base rates" at the same time that they are overly sensitive to the more vivid "target case" information

---

[1] In keeping with the findings of Grams and Schwab (1985) and McArthur and Obrant (1984), recent studies have failed to replicate Touhey's (1974a) finding that the rated prestige of an occupation is influenced by the percentage of women workers (e.g., Suchner, 1979; White et al., 1981).

concerning a particular individual (Nisbett and Ross, 1980). Consistent with this principle, the general information provided to analysts about the sex composition of the occupation seems to have no impact on job evaluations, while the specific information about the incumbent's gender has a strong effect.

Although the foregoing discussion provides some reason to be optimistic that a job's sex composition will not bias descriptions, caution must be exercised in extrapolating from the existing research to job evaluations in the real world. In particular, the experimental studies have manipulated information about sex-neutral jobs in order to create the impression that the percentage of women workers was high, moderate, or low. Sex composition effects may be much more potent when job descriptions are provided for occupations that are in fact filled predominately by workers of one sex or the other.

Since many job titles can reveal to people both the sex composition and the salary for the job that is being evaluated, the documented halo effects indicate the desirability of withholding such information from job analysts. Unfortunately, this is impossible when incumbents or their supervisors are providing job descriptions. Even when outside experts provide such descriptions, the information about job activities that they are given will often be sufficient to infer the job title and thus its salary and probable sex composition. Indeed, there is some evidence for the parallel effects of job activity descriptions and job titles on evaluations. Crowley (1981) found that subjects showed as much agreement regarding the status of various job activities as they did regarding the status of various job titles, and the activities elicited individual interest profiles that were just as sex-biased as those elicited by titles. While it thus seems unlikely that job descriptions could ever be generated by people who are unbiased by knowledge of the job's sex composition, prestige, and salary, it may be possible to conceal such information from those who use the job descriptions to evaluate the worth of the jobs on various compensable factors. As noted earlier, this phase of comparable worth analysis could even be performed by a computer, thereby ensuring that there is no halo bias.

It should be noted that a halo can be produced by more minor job attributes than salary or prestige. In particular, there is evidence to indicate that if the first piece of information provided in a social judgment task is positive, then evaluations of subsequent information will be more positively biased than those made when the first piece of information is negative. For example, evaluations of an individual's task performance were more positive when that person's initial performance was successful than when it was unsuccessful, even if the success rate was identical to those of other individuals (Jones and Goethals, 1972). This kind of primacy effect has important implications for the process of job analysis, since it is possible that early information will have disproportionate influence on job descriptions. If the initial information is highly positive, ratings on various descriptive dimensions may be positively inflated, whereas if the initial information is negative, these ratings may be negatively inflated. One way to deal with the problem is to instruct job analysts to attend equally to all pieces of information, since it has been found that such instructions can eliminate the primacy effect (Anderson and Hubert, 1963). Unfortunately, however, there is some evidence to suggest that with such instructions, a recency effect obtains—that is, judgments are overly influenced by later information. A second way to deal with this problem is to have the jobs systematically described by a number of raters, each of whom receives information about the job in a different order. Another kind of primacy halo concerns the order of the ratings as opposed to the order of the information. If the job yields highly positive ratings on the first descriptive dimension—e.g., mathematical skills required for the job— this positive impression may spill over onto subsequent dimensions—e.g., responsibility required by the job. Once again, this problem can be handled by having the jobs described by a number of raters, each of whom receives a different order of the rating dimensions.

The Expectancy Bias

Considerable evidence indicates that people's expectancies can exert an important influence on their social judgments. More specifically, people's judgments about the characteristics of other people tend to be overly influenced by information that confirms what they expect these characteristics to be (see McArthur, 1981, for a review of this literature). In the realm of job descriptions, an expectancy bias would be manifested in a tendency to describe a job with whatever characteristics are culturally expected for that job. Some evidence for this effect is provided in a study by Weiss and Shaw (1979), who found that workers' judgments regarding the motivating potential of various tasks were influenced not only by objective task differences but also by the attitudes of other workers toward the tasks. Such effects of social influence may also obtain for other judgments about jobs, such as the degree of various skills that they require or the negativity of the working conditions. The result may be that job descriptions reflect at least in part social stereotypes rather than the true nature of the jobs.

The influence of cultural expectations on job descriptions is particularly problematic when the goal is to describe accurately jobs that are segregated by sex. This is because attitudes toward men and women may influence descriptions of male and female jobs. There are widespread stereotypes concerning differences in ability and personality between men and women, stereotypes that are shared by members of both sexes. For example, in a now classic study, Broverman et al. (1972) found that a psychologically healthy woman, in comparison with a psychologically healthy man, was described by men and women alike as less independent, less competitive, less skilled in business, less of a leader, less ambitious, and less interested in math and science. On the positive side, a psychologically healthy woman was described as more tactful and more aware of others' feelings than was a psychologically healthy man.

Such sex stereotypes may well create assumptions regarding what abilities or personality traits are needed for women's work as opposed to men's work, and job descriptions provided by incumbents, supervisors, and experts may reflect these culturally shared expectations rather than reflecting the true requirements of a job. Thus, for example, there may be a bias against describing a woman's job as requiring a high degree of leadership or mathematical skill, as well as a bias against describing a man's work as requiring a high level of supervision or interpersonal sensitivity. Differential expectancies regarding the skills and abilities of men and women can bias job descriptions in another, more subtle way—namely, by influencing job analysts' causal attributions for successful task performance by men and women.

Considerable evidence indicates that for many tasks, men tend to attribute their successes to ability and their failures to bad luck, while women tend to do just the opposite, a difference that is due to men's greater expectancy for success (e.g., Deaux and Farris, 1977; Feather, 1969; Frieze, 1977). Moreover, when luck cannot reasonably be invoked to explain successful performance, women tend to attribute it to their high degree of effort, still eschewing ability as a cause. For example, a study of men and women in first-level management positions in a number of large organizations revealed that neither the women nor the men believed that luck had much to do with their success. Both sexes said that effort was responsible for their successful performance, but only men believed that ability was an equally important cause (Deaux, 1979).

It is not difficult to imagine how the tendency toward self-enhancement among men and self-deprecation among women borne of their differential expectancies for success could yield more favorable descriptions of jobs held predominately by men than those held predominately by women. One might suppose that using job descriptions from supervisors or expert analysts would circumvent the sex-linked biases that may enter into incumbent descriptions; unfortunately, this is not the case. Considerable research has revealed that the tendency for men to provide more self-enhancing explanations for their own successful performance than women do is paralleled in the explanations offered by outside observers, who also have stronger expectations that men will succeed (e.g., Deaux and Emswiller, 1974; Feather and Simon, 1975; Feldman-Summers and Kiesler, 1974).

While the foregoing arguments suggest that job descriptions will vary as a function of the worker's sex, a study by Rosenbach et al. (1979) found that male and female incumbents rated their jobs similarly on several important job dimensions, including the degree to which the job requires a variety of skills and the degree to which it provides autonomy in carrying out the work. However, there were some sex differences in job descriptions—e.g., women rated jobs lower in the degree to which they have a substantial impact on the lives or work of others. A major problem with this study is that the men and women from whom job descriptions were obtained did not occupy the same jobs. This is not so problematic for the authors' primary interest, which was relating job perceptions to job satisfaction. But it makes it very difficult to interpret similarities and differences in the actual content of job descriptions provided by men and women.

A study by Arvey et al. (1977) employed a methodology more appropriate to ascertaining the influence of sex-biased expectancies on job descriptions. These authors compared analysts' ratings of the same job when it was depicted with male and female incumbents in a verbal narrative accompanied by color slides. Although the results of this study revealed no effects of incumbents' sex on job descriptions, another study employing a videotaped depiction of jobs did find an effect of incumbents' sex (McArthur and Obrant, 1984). When jobs were depicted with male incumbents, analysts rated them as being relatively more critical to the company's assets and operations, as involving relatively more responsibility, and as having relatively less structure (i.e., fewer predetermined activities) than the same jobs depicted with female incumbents. These higher responsibility ratings for male-occupied jobs are consistent with sex-role stereotypes that paint the typical man as more skilled in business, more of a leader, more able to make decisions, and more independent than the typical woman (Broverman et al., 1972). Ratings of the skills required to perform the jobs provided less evidence of sex bias than did ratings of responsibility. While jobs depicted with male incumbents were perceived as requiring relatively more persuasive ability than those depicted with female incumbents—a finding consistent with the stereotype that men are more dominant than women—jobs depicted with male incumbents were not perceived to require more reasoning ability or more mathematical ability, thus providing no evidence for biasing effects of the stereotype that men are more logical and mathematically inclined than women.

Although procedural differences argue for the greater ecological validity of McArthur and Obrant's (1984) evidence of sex bias than the null findings of Arvey et al. (1977), additional research is clearly needed to establish the conditions under which job descriptions will be biased by sex-stereotyped cultural expectations. McArthur and Obrant's results suggest that such biases may be less pronounced in descriptions of a job's skill requirements than in descriptions of its responsibility. While the absence of gender bias in ratings of a job's skill is somewhat reassuring, it should be noted that responsibility has traditionally been a very important factor in job evaluations (Treiman, 1979), and the lesser responsibility ascribed to jobs depicted with female incumbents could yield an underestimation of the wages that women's work is worth. Indeed, McArthur and Obrant (1984) found that jobs depicted with female incumbents were rated by analysts as meriting relatively lower wages than the same jobs depicted with male incumbents.

While the absence of sex bias in analysts' ratings of the skills required by jobs clearly provides no assurance of unbiased ratings of comparable worth, it does provide some suggestions regarding how to generate job evaluations that are not biased by the incumbent's sex. More specifically, the absence of sex bias in most skill ratings may be due to the fact that people have become sensitized to sexism in judging abilities, with the consequence that analysts deliberately attended to information indicative of skilled work by female incumbents. This interpretation suggests that raising people's awareness of sexism in judging responsibility may reduce the sex bias in ratings on this dimension as well. The lesser sex bias in ratings of skill than in ratings of responsibility may also be due to the fact that evaluating the skills required of a job is a more objective task and thus less subject to the expectancy bias. This possibility suggests that providing raters with more explicit criteria regarding what constitutes a job with high responsibility, low structure, or high criticality could reduce sex bias in these ratings by virtue of guiding attention to the relevant as opposed to the expected information.

While careful instructions to job analysts may help to reduce sex bias, the ideal solution to the expectancy bias would be to conceal the incumbent's sex during the process of job analysis. As noted earlier, the incumbent's sex could be concealed during evaluations of a job's worth on various compensable factors by employing a computer programmed to allocate some predetermined worth or job points for each element in the job description. However, to conceal the incumbent's sex during the process of job description is more problematic. One possibility would be to provide written information about the jobs for analysts to use in generating job descriptions on a structured instrument like the PAQ. The question is, who will provide the written information and will the information be the same for male and female incumbents? Even if it is the same, it is likely that the analysts will envision incumbents of one or another gender when rating a job and, according to the availability bias, the gender of the incumbent they envision will be whichever one is the most frequent in that particular occupation. Another possibility would be for the incumbents to describe their own jobs on a structured questionnaire. Unfortunately, as noted earlier, there is considerable evidence to indicate that the sex biases manifested in observers' judgments about male and female workers are paralleled in the judgments offered by the workers themselves.

Given the difficulty of concealing the sex of incumbents, it may be advisable to obtain structured ratings of all jobs from incumbents of a single sex. In the absence of information regarding whose descriptions are the most accurate, either male or female workers could be selected so long as workers of the same sex are used for all jobs whose worth is to be compared. A problem arises, however, when descriptions are sought for the large majority of occupations that are filled predominately by workers of one sex or the other. It is possible that the descriptions provided by a male secretary, for example, would not be representative of secretaries in general. Despite the null effect of sex composition in past research, it is also possible that the sex composition of highly segregated occupations could bias job descriptions even when the sex of the incumbents who are viewed is held constant.

DEFINING THE COMPENSABLE FACTORS

As noted earlier, evaluating the comparable worth of jobs requires determining which job elements should be compensated rather than relying on market indicators of which job elements are currently compensated. Like job descriptions and evaluations, the choice of compensable factors and their weights is necessarily a subjective judgment that is vulnerable to the judgmental biases discussed above.

Most job analysis procedures have employed a relatively small set of factors deemed as legitimate bases for pay differentials: skills, experience, responsibility, effort, and working conditions. While these factors have some face validity, they nevertheless represent value judgments and should not be accepted without question. One question is: Who should make the judgment? When employees are organized, the decision could be made through collective bargaining. However, it is not clear what should be done when employees are not organized. It is entirely possible that having the employer make the decision could yield weighted compensable factors that ultimately serve to justify lower wages for certain categories of "women's work" than for "men's work." This may result not so much from deliberate discrimination on the part of the employer as from the likelihood that the employer's choices will be vulnerable to judgmental biases.

The availability heuristic could bias the choice of compensable factors, since the bases for pay differentials that most readily come to mind may be those that are the most frequent in the work world. Halo effects could also bias the choice of compensable factors, since the factors that are designated may be those that are evaluatively consistent with financial rewards. The consequence of this will be that the positive aspects of jobs will be viewed as meriting compensation, while negative job elements will be given little weight. It should be noted that both the availability heuristic and the halo effect favor compensable factors that would legitimize the current wage structure. Consider, for example, the occupation of child care. The availability heuristic will generate compensable factors that are the most frequent bases for pay differentials, such as special skills and training and responsibility for other workers or money. Since these factors are not highly represented in child care, they will serve to justify its poor compensation. In addition, halo effects will militate against compensating "negative" factors, such as little opportunity for advancement, little job security, and a nonoptimal level of difficulty (relatively easy and boring), all of which are highly represented in child care. By traditional yardsticks, then, child care will not be viewed as comparable in worth to, say, dentistry. But if one considers the worth of these two jobs by another yardstick—such as what would happen in our society if nobody engaged in child care versus what would happen if nobody engaged in dentistry—then clearly the women's work of child care is of greater worth to society.

The question remains as to what can be done to guard against biases in the choice and weighting of compensable factors that may devalue the worth of jobs held primarily by one sex or the other. Ideally, one would like to have some objective criterion for evaluating the legitimacy of a designated basis for pay differentials. The next best thing would be to establish a broad-based subjective criterion. For example, surveys could be conducted to ascertain employers' and employees' beliefs regarding the legitimate bases for pay differentials as well as how these bases should be weighted in fixing wages. One would hope to find a consensus regarding at least some compensable factors. However, the small amount of relevant research on this subject suggests that the choice of compensable factors will vary across jobs as well as across job analysts.

McArthur and Obrant (1984) found that those job description measures that were significantly related to analysts' ratings of a job's monetary worth varied as a function of the job and as a function of the worker's gender. Most notably, there were no significant predictors of the monetary worth of jobs depicted with female incumbents. It should be noted that this study did not directly ask job analysts to indicate what job elements should be compensated. Rather, regression analyses were employed to determine empirically which job elements predicted ratings of monetary worth. One might hope that direct assessment of analysts' beliefs regarding what elements should be compensated would yield more thoughtful and thus consistent responses.

However, several surveys have revealed that people's responses to the questions "What aspects of jobs do you think should be compensated?" and "How important should each factor be in determining salary?" varied as a function of the particular job they were considering as well as their own job (McArthur et al., 1984).

The apparent lack of consensus regarding what job factors should be compensated presents a very serious problem for comparable worth analyses, and additional research is clearly needed to determine whether the preliminary findings reported here are reliable. In conducting this research, it is important that judgments be obtained regarding the legitimacy of a large variety of bases for pay differentials, not just those that have been commonly employed in existing job analyses. In particular, potentially compensable factors that are embodied in "women's work" need to be identified and included along with the more standard factors to see how they stack up in people's judgments regarding the legitimate bases for pay differentials. Also, factors that have been shown to influence how worthwhile a job is to the employee should be rated. These include the opportunity for advancement, job security, and job difficulty (Jurgensen, 1978; Walker et al., 1982). In a sense these factors represent an expansion of the standard factor of working conditions, and the implication of including them is that jobs may be worth higher wages not only if the physical working conditions are poor but also if the psychological conditions are poor.[2]

CONCLUSIONS

The complexity and inherent subjectivity of job analysis coupled with the limitations of human judgment make it extremely unlikely that the objectively true worth of jobs can ever be established, even if some consensus could be reached regarding what job elements should be compensated. The inevitable biases in job descriptions would not be so problematic for comparable worth analysis if one could assume that they were not sex-linked: if judgmental biases simply added a constant error to evaluations of every job, the true relative standing of men's and women's jobs would be maintained. Unfortunately, however, the evidence reviewed in this paper provides considerable reason for concern that judgmental biases are weighted in the direction of underestimating the wages that women's work is worth relative to that of men. The halo bias will overestimate the worth of work that is

---

[2] While one might expect that the allocation of higher wages in compensation for these poor working conditions would find considerable support, this does run contrary to halo effects. And it should be recalled that, consistent with a positive halo effect, McArthur and Obrant (1984) found that the more desirable a job was, the greater was its judged monetary worth.

relatively prestigious and well paid—men's work. The expectancy bias will overestimate the skills, leadership, training, and effort that are required by work that is culturally expected to require such qualities—men's work. And the availability bias will reinforce this tendency, inasmuch as it will overestimate the frequency of familiar—i.e., expected—job activities, in addition to those that are recent or perceptually salient.

Given the difficulty of removing certain biases from job descriptions, it would seem advisable to conduct research designed to determine how to best reduce their influence. Providing raters with very explicit criteria regarding what aspects of a job merit what ratings on structured job description instruments might help to reduce bias. Alerting job analysts to their potential biases may also help. Finally, research comparing the job descriptions provided by incumbents, supervisors, and experts can identify the source of job descriptions that are the least sex-biased.

While research can determine the conditions that minimize sex biases, it can never prove that such biases will be absent from comparable worth analyses. This is because most jobs are sex-segregated. When the same job is occupied by men and by women, one can compare the job descriptions provided by different sources (incumbents, supervisors, and experts) under various instructional conditions and determine whether descriptions vary as a function of the incumbent's sex. If they do not, one can conclude that there is no sex bias given a particular source and a particular set of instructions. However, when a job is occupied primarily by incumbents of one sex, it is virtually impossible to determine whether descriptions vary as a function of the incumbent's sex, and it is thus impossible to ensure that the job description is not sex-biased. In such instances, the best one can do is to choose the source of job descriptions and set of instructions that provide the most similar descriptions of jobs whether the incumbent is male or female. It must be noted, however, that the absence of sex bias in descriptions of jobs that are not sex-linked may not be generalizable to descriptions of jobs that are sex-linked. For example, even if female bank tellers describe their jobs as requiring the same amount of physical effort as male tellers do, this does not ensure that female typists' descriptions of the physical effort entailed in their work will not be underestimated compared with male truck drivers' descriptions of their own physical effort.

An alternative to eliminating or reducing sex biases in job descriptions would be to attempt to compensate for them. For example, if one found that female incumbents underestimate the physical effort required by a particular job in comparison with male incumbents, then some constant factor could be added to female incumbents' estimates of effort required in other jobs—jobs for which there are few male incumbents. However, such a strategy assumes a constant sex bias in job descriptions, and this assumption may well be wrong. Another strategy for dealing with sex biases in job descriptions is to attempt to employ at least some objective measures. For example, the physical effort required by a job could conceivably be assessed with some kind of mechanical device. Similarly, the working conditions could be objectively described via indices of temperature, square footage per worker, and so forth. Such measures are, of course, limited in scope as well as being more costly and cumbersome to employ than subjective judgments are.

While research may provide methods for reducing judgmental biases in comparable worth analysis, it is likely that such biases will never be completely eliminated. As a result, comparable worth analyses may well yield an underestimation of the wages that women's work is worth, thereby redressing only a portion of the existing wage gap. This in itself is not so bad. What is more worrisome is the likelihood that any remaining gender gap in wages would be certified as just. Whether or not the benefits of the first outcome outweigh the risks of the second is an important question to consider in deciding whether comparable worth analysis is better than alternative methods, such as unionizing and collective bargaining, for reducing wage inequities.

REFERENCES

Anderson, N.H., and S. Hubert
   1983   Effects of concomitant verbal recall on order effects in personality impression formation. *Journal of Personality and Social Psychology* 2:379-391.
Arvey, R.D., E.M. Passino, and J.W. Lounsbury
   1977   Job analysis results as influenced by sex of incumbent and sex of analyst. *Journal of Applied Psychology* 62:411-416.
Broverman, I.K., S.R. Vogel, D.M. Broverman, F.E. Clarkson, and P.S. Rosenkrantz
   1972   Sex-role stereotypes and clinical judgments of mental health. *Journal of Social Issues* 28:59-78.
Crowley, A.D.
   1981   The content of interest inventories: Job titles or job activities? *Journal of Occupational Psychology* 54:135-140.
Deaux, K.
   1979   Self-evaluation of male and female managers. *Sex Roles* 5:571-580.
Deaux, K., and T. Emswiller
   1974   Explanations of successful performance on sex-linked tasks: What's skill for the male is luck for the female. *Journal of Personality and Social Psychology* 29:80-85.
Deaux, K., and E. Farris
   1977   Attributing causes for one's own performance: The effects of sex, norms, and outcome. *Journal of Research Personality* 11:59-72.
Desmond, R., and D. Weiss
   1973   Supervisor estimation of abilities required in jobs. *Journal of Vocational Behavior* 3:181-194.
   1975   Worker estimation of abilities required in jobs. *Journal of Vocational Behavior* 5:145-158.

Feather, N.T.
  1969   Attribution of responsibility and valence of success and failure in relation to initial
          confidence and task performance. *Journal of Personality and Social Psychology*
          13:129–144.
Feather, N.T., and J.G. Simon
  1975   Reactions to male and female success and failure in sex-linked occupations: Impressions
          of personality, causal attribution, and perceived likelihood of different consequences.
          Journal of Personality and Social Psychology 31:20–31.
Feldman-Summers, S., and S.B. Kiesler
  1974   Those who are number two try harder: The effect of sex on attributions of causality.
          Journal of Personality and Social Psychology 30:846–855.
Fischer, D.G., and J. Sobkow
  1979   Workers' estimation of ability requirements of their jobs. *Perceptual and Motor Skills*
          48:519–531.
Frieling, E.
  1977   Occupational analysis: Some details of an illustrative German project. *International
          Review of Applied Psychology* 26:77–85.
Frieze, I.H.
  1977   Women's expectations for and causal attributions of success and failure. In M. Mednick,
          S.S. Tangri, and L. Hoffman, eds., *Women and Achievement: Social and Motivational
          Analyses*. Washington, D.C.: Hemisphere.
Grams, R., and D.P. Schwab
  1985   Systematic sex-related error in job evaluation. *Academy of Management Journal* (Forth-
          coming).
Griffen, R.W.
  1981   A longitudinal investigation of task characteristics relationships. *Academy of Manage-
          ment Journal* 24:99–113.
Jones, E.E., and G.R. Goethals
  1972   Order effects in impression formation: Attribution context and the nature of the entity.
          Pp. 79–94 in E.E. Jones, D.E. Kanouse, H.H. Kelley, R.E. Nisbett, S. Valins, and B.
          Weiner, eds., *Attribution: Perceiving the Causes of Behavior*. Morristown, N.J.: Gen-
          eral Learning Press.
Jurgensen, C.E.
  1978   Job preferences (What makes a job good or bad?). *Journal of Applied Psychology*
          63:267–276.
Kelley, H.H.
  1950   The warm cold variable in first impressions of persons. *Journal of Personality* 18:431–
          439.
McArthur, L.Z.
  1981   What grabs you: The role of attention in impression formation and causal attribution. In
          E.T. Higgins, C.P. Herman, and M.P. Zanna, eds., *Social Cognition: The Ontario
          Symposium*. Vol. 1. Hillsdale, N.J.: Erlbaum.
McArthur, L.Z., and S. Obrant
  1984   Sex Biases in Comparable Worth Analysis. Unpublished research, Department of Psy-
          chology, Brandeis University.
McArthur, L.Z., J. Karas, J. Neri, A. Pressel, and D. Rudin
  1984   Choosing Compensable Factors for Comparable Worth Analysis. Unpublished paper,
          Department of Psychology, Brandeis University.
McCormick, E.J., P.R. Jeanneret, and R.C. Meacham
  1969   Position Analysis Questionnaire. Purdue Research Foundation, West Lafayette, Ind.

1972   A study of job characteristics and job dimensions as based on the Position Analysis Questionnaire (PAQ). *Journal of Applied Psychology Monograph* 56:347–368.

Narayanan, S., and R. Venkatachalam
1982   Perception of organizational climate. *Perceptual and Motor Skills* 55:15–18.

Nisbett, R.E., and L. Ross
1980   *Human Inference: Strategies and Shortcomings of Social Judgment.* Englewood Cliffs, N.J.: Prentice-Hall.

Rosenbach, W.E., R.C. Dailey, and C.P. Morgan
1979   Perceptions of job characteristics and affective work outcomes for women and men. *Sex Roles* 5:267–277.

Ross, M.
1981   Self-centered biases in attributions of responsibility: Antecedents and consequences. In E.T. Higgins, C.P. Herman, and M.P. Zanna, eds., *Social Cognition: The Ontario Symposium.* Vol. 1. Hillsdale, N.J.: Erlbaum.

Suchner, R.W.
1979   Sex ratios and occupational prestige: Three failures to replicate a sexist bias. *Personality and Social Psychology Bulletin* 5:236–239.

Touhey, J.C.
1974a   Effects of additional women professionals on ratings of occupational prestige and desirability. *Journal of Personality and Social Psychology* 29:86–89.
1974b   Effects of additional men on prestige and desirability of occupations typically performed by women. *Journal of Applied Social Psychology* 4:330–332.

Treiman, D.J.
1979   *Job Evaluation: An Analytic Review.* Committee on Occupational Classification and Analysis. Washington, D.C.: National Academy of Sciences.

Treiman, D.J., and H.I. Hartmann, eds.
1981   *Women, Work, and Wages: Equal Pay for Jobs of Equal Value.* Committee on Occupational Classification and Analysis. Washington, D.C.: National Academy Press.

Tversky, A., and D. Kahneman
1974   Judgment under uncertainty: Heuristics and biases. *Science* 185:1124–1131.

Walker, J.E., C. Tausky, and D. Oliver
1982   Men and women at work: Similarities and differences in work values within occupational groupings. *Journal of Vocational Behavior* 21:17–36.

Weiss, H.M., and J.B. Shaw
1979   Social influences on judgments about tasks. *Organizational Behavior and Human Performance* 24:126–140.

White, M.C., M.D. Crino, and G.L. DeSanctis
1981   Ratings of prestige and desirability: Effects of additional women entering selected business occupations. *Personality and Social Psychology Bulletin* 7:588–592.

The Economic Case
for Comparable Worth

Barbara R. Bergmann

Those concerned to find the most expeditious cure for the huge disadvantage of women in terms of the average wages they receive have fixed their attention on the idea that employers should be required or encouraged to make changes in the pattern of occupational wages. Such changes would be designed to bring wages in predominantly female occupations and wages in predominantly male occupations closer together. These occupational wage changes might be made legislatively or administratively in public employment, might be made through collective bargaining in unionized establishments, or might be ordered by judges as remedies in cases of sex discrimination under Title VII of the Civil Rights Act of 1964.

This paper examines some of the issues associated with wage changes designed to reduce the wage gap between the sexes: When, if ever, and on what grounds might such wage changes be made? What kind of system might be used in arriving at the new wage structure? Are the slogans "comparable pay for jobs of comparable worth" and "pay equity" useful in this context or do they muddy the waters?

An economist is, almost by definition, a person elaborately trained to demonstrate and to preach that prices and wages are best determined in a free, competitive market by supply and demand. Any economist who would urge on fellow economists the desirability of enforced and administered revisions to wages has a heavy burden of proof to bear. If she or he goes further to suggest that considerations of worth or equity have some validity, the burden becomes even heavier. This paper is an attempt to shoulder some of that burden.

The main line of argument is the rather obvious one that the market in which occupational wages are set lacks important elements of freedom and competition. In the future, after sex (and race) discrimination have been eliminated, the pattern of occupational wages will be determined in a market that is more free and more competitive. The wage structure that then results from the interplay of supply and demand will surely look very different from the existing one, because the supply of and the demand for labor in each occupation will no longer be affected by discrimination as they now are.

I further argue that wage revisions designed to reduce the wage gap between the sexes are reasonable and desirable if they bring us closer to the more efficient and fairer wage structure that would be established by the free market itself in the absence of discrimination. The goal of research in this area must be the construction of methodologies to estimate in some detail what the postdiscrimination pattern of wages will look like. As we shall see, this will involve descriptions of jobs in terms of the qualifications a person must have to perform them successfully. Conventional job evaluations, as currently developed, may well meet many of the desiderata of such models, although this is a matter for further research.

The paper starts out with a case so simple that it contains none of the complications involved in the implementation of wage realignment in any real situation. This simple case, however, does lay out the bare bones of the rationale for such realignment when discrimination is an important element in the marketplace. In this case I demonstrate that applying the labels "pay equity" or "comparable worth" to the principles advanced to justify and guide such a realignment does not strain economic sense. The subsequent discussion is designed to deal with some, although far from all, of the difficulties posed by more realistic cases, in which factors other than discrimination come into play.

A VERY SIMPLIFIED, TWO-OCCUPATION CASE

I start by considering the obviously unrealistic case in which differences in training, native abilities, and tastes for different kinds of work are assumed to play no part. In analyzing a labor market with just two occupations, I initially assume that anyone in the labor market, male or female, is capable of doing either job equally well and likes one job as well as the other.

It is most convenient and sacrifices no generality to consider the argument in terms of a numerical example. While such an example has the disadvantage of wearying most readers with discussion on an elementary level, it has the countervailing advantage of providing fairly realistic numerical estimates of the costs of wage realignment for use in later sections.

Table 1 gives in numerical form hypothetical demand schedules for the

TABLE 1   Illustrative Demand Schedules

Occupation A		Occupation B		Total Demand (under assumption of equal wages)	
Weekly Wage	Number of Workers Demanded (thousands)	Weekly Wage	Number of Workers Demanded (thousands)	Weekly Wage in Both Occupations	Number of Workers Demanded (thousands)
$300	8	$300	0	$300	8
250	11	250	1	250	12
200	14	200	4	200	18
150	17	150	7	150	24
100	20	100	10	100	30

two occupations, which represent the number of workers that employers would hire for those jobs at various wage levels. For example, at a wage of $200 per week, employers in this labor market are assumed to be willing to hire 14,000 workers in occupation A. At the same wage in occupation B they are assumed to want to hire 4,000, for a total of 18,000. At higher wages, employers would want to hire fewer workers, and at lower wages it is assumed they would want to hire more.

Hypothetical supply schedules by sex are displayed in Table 2, which shows the numbers of men and women who would offer their labor to employers at various wage rates.

The Case of No Sex Discrimination

Let us first assume that employers act on a sex-neutral basis and welcome men and women into both occupations. Under this assumption, market

TABLE 2   Illustrative Supply Schedules

Men		Women		Total Supply	
Weekly Wage	Number of Workers Supplied (thousands)	Weekly Wage	Number of Workers Supplied (thousands)	Weekly Wage in Both Occupations	Number of Workers Supplied in Both Occupations (thousands)
$300	12	$300	10	$300	22
250	11	250	9	250	20
200	10	200	8	200	18
150	9	150	7	150	16
100	8	100	6	100	14

forces would be expected to eliminate any difference in wages between occupation A and occupation B. If any difference in wages did show up, workers in the lower-paid occupation would try to shift to the higher-paid occupation. I am assuming there would be no bar to such movement because of lack of training or skill, distaste for the occupation, or custom. Nor are employers assumed at this point to inhibit the flow of workers by excluding anyone for reasons of sex. The attempt of workers to enter the higher-paying occupation would increase the supply of workers to it and would decrease the supply of workers to the lower-paying occupation. This would go on until the wages in the two occupations were once again in equality.

Since wages in the two occupations can, under these assumptions, be assumed to be the same, except for temporary lapses, it makes sense to compile a "total demand" schedule, which is the total amount of labor that employers would be willing to hire at various wage levels with identical wages in the two occupations. This schedule is displayed in the last two columns of Table 1.

If wages do not differ by sex, it makes further sense to compile a "total supply" schedule of people available to employers at each wage. This schedule is shown on the right in Table 2.

In the hypothesized case, because there is competition across the sexes for jobs and across jobs for labor, the considerations of supply and demand would suggest that the wage in both occupations and for both sexes would be $200 a week. This is the wage at which the number of workers sought by employers would be equal to the number of workers who wanted jobs in each occupation and in the labor market as a whole. This solution is shown diagrammatically in Figure 1. There would be 14,000 people in jobs of type A and 4,000 in jobs of type B, and the wage would be the same in both jobs. Both men's and women's wages would be $200. In such a labor market, we would expect to see men and women in both occupations.

The Case of Sex Segregation of Occupations

Let us now change the assumptions about how employers operate and assume that they maintain the practice of restricting women to jobs in occupation B. I will continue to assume that men and women do not differ in skill or in preferences for one job over another. I will not pause here to discuss the possible reasons that employers might pursue such a policy, which would have to be labeled discriminatory by any reasonable definition of that term, given the assumptions. Nor shall I examine the issue of whether competitive pressures would allow employers to persist in such behavior. Some economists and sociologists see the actual labor market as operating to an impor-

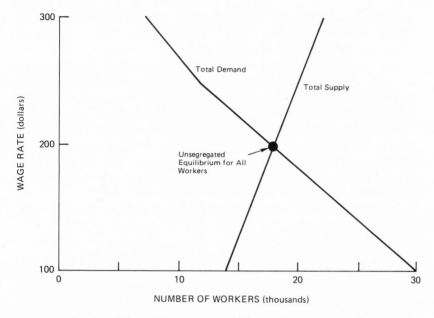

FIGURE 1   Supply and demand in unsegregated labor markets.

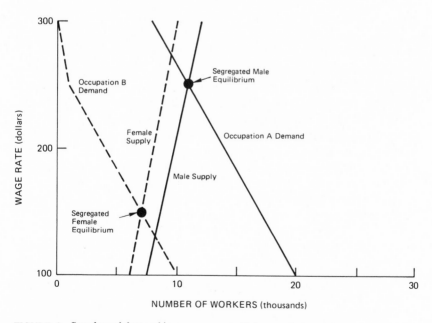

FIGURE 2   Supply and demand in sex-segregated labor markets.

tant extent in the way I assume in this case, but others, of course, do not.[1] For readers in the latter camp, the arguments of this paper will be acceptable, if at all, only as applying to an unrealistic case.

Whatever the psychological or sociological or economic reasons for employers to insist on the posited sex segregation of occupations, the supply and demand resulting from their behavior would be very different from that in a labor market in which occupational sex segregation was absent and employers paid no attention to sex, as under the assumptions in the previous section. The demand schedule for occupation A would become simply the demand schedule for male workers, and similarly the demand schedule for occupation B would become the demand schedule for female workers. It would no longer be appropriate to add up the demand schedules or the supply schedules into unified market schedules, because occupational segregation has changed the structure of the labor market so that the market does not operate in a unified way.

Instead, there are now separate men's and women's labor markets, each with an independent wage determination process. In fact, going back to the numerical example in Tables 1 and 2, the supply and demand conditions now assumed to be in force would dictate that the market for men would be cleared at an average wage of $250 per week, and the market for women cleared at $150.[2] This outcome is displayed in Figure 2.

WAGE STRUCTURES IN INDIVIDUAL ESTABLISHMENTS

My analysis has thus far encompassed the labor market as a whole. At this point let us shift the focus to the individual employer and inquire how this employer participates in the labor market and is affected by it.

An employer whose establishment has jobs in particular occupations will keep cognizant of the market wage for workers considered to be acceptable for performing those occupations. The employer will keep abreast of what other employers are paying such workers—and use that information in setting the firm's wages for jobs in those occupations. To an employer who practices sex segregation, being of the correct sex is a requirement for acceptability in each occupation, along with the ability to do the job.

---

[1] Gold (1983) presents arguments on both sides of the case.

[2] The argument adopted here closely resembles the line taken in Bergmann (1971). In addition, it is argued in Bergmann and Darity (1981) that occupational segregation may have an economic motivation in that it prevents difficult social situations from arising in the workplace and so enhances productivity in the short run.

The reason for an employer's use of information about what other employers are paying to "acceptable" workers lies in the employer's own interest. If an establishment sets a wage for an occupation much below what other employers are offering, few acceptable workers may apply, and the establishment's best workers may leave. If an establishment's wage is set much above the market wage—the average that others are paying—costs may be unnecessarily driven above and profits driven below what they might otherwise have been.

In some situations an establishment may want to depart from the market wage. Sometimes the offer of a wage similar to the market wage brings too few acceptable applicants; the firm must then consider whether the productivity of this type of worker is high enough to make it profitable to offer a higher wage. In the opposite case, when there is an oversupply of acceptable applicants, a lower wage may be set, at least for new entrants. Situations like this, in which firms depart from market wages, change the levels of market wages and make them responsive to changes in the conditions of supply of workers to firms and the demand by firms for workers.

In the presence of competition it makes economic sense for employers to pay attention to the market wage when setting their own wages and—in the absence of discrimination—it is generally conducive to economic efficiency that firms operate in this way.

Let us now consider how individual firms that have entry-level jobs in occupations A and B might react to market wages when, as in the example in the previous section, these wages have been influenced by other employers' segregation of male and female workers. Let us assume as above that all men and women in the labor market from which the company draws its workers are capable of doing all the jobs and, given equal pay, would be indifferent to which job they held.

Wages in a Nondiscriminating Firm

Let us first consider the situation of the Smith Company, which I will assume is the exception to the general practice of sex segregation and, unlike other employers, does not take into account the sex of the applicant in deciding whether to hire and where to place that applicant. We may now ask what wages Smith Company might reasonably set.

One possibility for Smith would be to ascertain market wages for both occupations and to set wages as other employers do. This behavior would set the jobs held by men in other companies (occupation A) at a higher rate of pay than jobs held by women in other companies (occupation B). Smith Company would, with that conventional wage structure, end up with both men and women in occupation A—the male-type jobs—and all or mostly women in occupation B—the female-type jobs. Men applying to Smith who were not offered occupation A jobs could probably do better elsewhere, and few would accept employment by Smith in occupation B jobs. As time went on, the women employed by Smith in occupation B jobs would ask for transfers to the occupation A jobs in Smith, and, if they were given preference over outside applicants, these jobs would also become all female.

If the nondiscriminating Smith Company did mimic the wage practices of discriminating companies, it would not be maximizing its profit, however. The supply situation faced by Smith for occupation A would be different from that faced by the discriminating companies by virtue of the fact that Smith considers women as well as men to be acceptable for those jobs. Smith would have a surplus of candidates for jobs in occupation A, and the principles outlined above should lead Smith to lower the wage it offers in that occupation. In fact, Smith would end up paying about the same in occupations A and B. The wage for both would be the wage paid for B by discriminating employers. In so doing Smith would cut its labor cost by eliminating the bonus paid in occupation A jobs—a bonus made unnecessary by the successful recruitment of women into them. In this case we would expect to see few men in any of Smith's entry-level jobs.[3]

It should be noted that profit-maximizing behavior for Smith with respect to wage structure would be to install for its own internal use the wage structure that would be general in the market in the absence of discrimination. To the extent that Smith's nondiscriminatory behavior has an appreciable influence on market wages, the effect will be to reduce the differential between wages in occupations A and B paid by firms that continue to discriminate because of the decreased employment of men and the increased employment of women by Smith. This would increase the supply of men and decrease the supply of women to other employers. Thus, the more Smith Companies we have, the lower will be the average differential between wages in the two occupations in the market generally.

Wages in a Discriminating Firm

Let us contrast the situation at Smith Company with that of Jones Company, which considers only men to be acceptable in occupation A. Given

---

[3] Empirical evidence that this analysis is correct is found in Blau (1976). In examining the hiring and wage practices of employers of white-collar labor, she found that some companies hired only men in some job types. Companies that allowed women into those occupations paid workers in those jobs considerably less than did companies that excluded women.

I also note here that economist Allen Greenspan is reported to employ practices in his consulting business similar to those of the Smith Company in the example. He said to a *New York Times* interviewer that he hires women economists and pays them less than he would have to pay men of equivalent quality.

that Jones will not allow women into A, it maximizes its profit subject to this self-imposed constraint on whom it can hire in each occupation. To do this it mimics the wage structure of other employers, the vast majority of whom maintain a similar segregated pattern. Jones cannot hire enough acceptable workers for occupation A unless it pays the high wages that its discriminating rivals do, and Jones need pay only the customary low wages for occupation B to maintain an adequate supply of women to such jobs.

This is a good place to observe that while occupational segregation is surely a cause of wage differentials between men and women, causation may also (and at the same time) run in the other direction. The desire on the part of an employer like Jones to maintain a wage structure like that of other employers—i.e., to pay market wages—may enhance the desire to maintain occupational segregation, even in the absence of discriminatory feelings. If a female job candidate is allowed by an employer who pays market wages to chose between vacancies in occupation A and occupation B, the employer will have trouble filling the lower-paying occupation B jobs. To avoid this the employer must steer female candidates to jobs in occupation B by hints that they will get no job at all if they insist on a job in occupation A.

WAGE REALIGNMENT IN THE SIMPLE CASE

Let us proceed by assuming that a federal judge has seen evidence of the occupational segregation of men and women at Jones Company and has been presented with evidence that their qualifications do not differ. Under the Civil Rights Act, the judge has ordered the company not only to cease barring women from occupation A, but also to realign its wage structure.[4] We must now consider whether there is a way to realign wage rates in the Jones Company that does less violence to economic logic than the current setup does.

Standard economic theory teaches that efficiency is promoted when commodities substitutable on a one-for-one basis (all male and female workers, in the example) have the same price. When employers discriminate, this principle is violated. The most obvious principle to use in realigning wage rates in the Jones Company is to arrange matters so that, within the firm, substitutable workers have the same wages.[5]

In following this principle and equalizing the wages of Jones Company workers in occupations A and B, one would, of course, be creating a new inequality in the wages of substitutable workers—namely, between workers

---

[4] For a discussion of some of the legal issues in the context of the economic issues, see Bergmann and Gray (1984). An earlier version of some of the material used in this paper appears there.

[5] What an appropriate definition of "substitutable" might be in this context is briefly discussed in the next section.

employed by Jones and workers employed by companies that continue to follow the market currently dominated by discriminating employers. It is the potential creation of this new type of inequality (together with a preference for market processes over administrative processes) that probably accounts for the strength of the opposition of many economists to the wage realignment urged by the advocates of comparable worth.

The proposed exchange of one type of inequality for another is not, however, an exchange that moves us backward or leaves us static in terms of equity and efficiency. On the contrary, in addition to moving us forward in terms of equity, such an exchange also moves us forward toward the achievement of a wage structure for the market as a whole in which the principle of equality of wages for substitutable workers is in force. As more establishments voluntarily or involuntarily realign, average practice will become more like that in realigned establishments, and the market will be closer to the nondiscriminatory wage structure blessed as efficient by economic theory.

In arriving at the conclusion that Jones Company ought, under our simplified assumptions, to be required to pay equal wages in occupations A and B, we did not need to know anything about the duties or "value to the employer" of the two occupations. The assumption that all members of the labor force can do both jobs equally well and do not prefer one job over the other is sufficient for this result, because this condition implies that a nondiscriminatory market would have resulted in equal wages in the two occupations. As the next section shows, considerably weaker assumptions as to substitutability will also suffice.

The notions of comparable worth and pay equity were not really needed to arrive at this understanding. However, it is worth remarking that after wages in the example are aligned so that they are equal, the rational employer will equate the marginal productivities in the two occupations, so that the "worth" to the employer of the (equally capable) marginal workers in both occupations will be comparable and, indeed, will be equal. Moreover, the realignment clearly increases fairness. So those who would apply the terms "comparable worth" and "pay equity" to this process of realigning wages are not being misleading in any fundamental sense. The worst that might be said of the terms is that they are needlessly provoking to neoclassical economists.

What should the level of the newly equalized wages be? We must assume that the Jones Company is already a going concern. If Jones Company is typical, about 60 percent of its incumbent workers are men in A-type jobs at $250 and 40 percent are women in B-type jobs at $150.

If Jones is allowed or forced to do what the Smith Company has done voluntarily, the Jones male workers will have to take a very sizable pay cut. This may be judged unfair to them, may cause the company to suffer high

THE ECONOMIC CASE FOR COMPARABLE WORTH

turnover, and may be legally and politically impossible. If, however, the women in occupation B are brought up to the level of $250, then, using the numerical illustration, the company will have a 27 percent increase in its payroll, a development possibly fraught with heavy repercussions for the company's profitability. The profitability problems would be especially severe if Jones is the only company whose wages are being realigned and if Jones served a small share of a relatively competitive product market. If, however, Jones is a state government, the danger of having to cease operations would be absent.

One possible compromise would be to have a period of a few years in which wages in occupation A would rise by a considerably smaller percentage than wages in occupation B. For example, in a year in which all wages went up an average of 10 percent, occupation A wages could rise by 2 percent while occupation B wages rose by 30 percent. This would lower the wage gap between A and B from $100 to $65, or 45 percent in a single year.

After the Jones Company had realigned its wages, the pattern of its occupational wages would look very different from the pattern in the market consisting of the remainder of the companies that exclude women from certain jobs. As time went on, however, and more of these companies went through the wage realignment process, reduced occupational segregation, and increased their demand for women workers to take jobs in previously male occupations, the wage patterns in the nonrealigned companies might be expected to move toward those in the realigned companies, as the latter came to dominate the market.

ABILITIES, TASTES, AND SUBSTITUTABILITY

Up to this point, the discussion has proceeded under the assumption that workers do not differ in terms of their ability or desire with respect to the two occupations into which I have assumed they are divided. These assumptions led to the conclusion that in a nondiscriminatory labor market, wages in the two occupations would be equal. This in turn suggested that, within firms, wages in the two occupations should be equalized.

In fact, in order to arrive at the conclusion that wages in the two occupations should be equalized within firms, it is not necessary to assume that all women could hold and would be willing to hold jobs that are currently dominated by men.[6] A considerably weaker assumption would do. Just enough women need to be willing and able to change occupations so that the "crowding" of labor in the women's occupations would be relieved if

---

[6] The material in this section originates in a discussion I had with Mark Killingsworth, who is not, however, to be construed as agreeing with the point of view taken in this paper.

employer-enforced segregation were relaxed. In the numerical example, starting from a condition of complete segregation, a shift of just half the women from occupation B to occupation A would accomplish this. What the necessary proportion would be in reality and whether skills and tastes are or might soon be such as to allow for a large enough shift on the part of women into male-dominated occupations are questions that only empirical research or the future course of events can answer.

The assumption of substitutability can also be relaxed somewhat with no violence to the conclusions. A contention, for example, that typists and truck drivers might get the same pay in a nondiscriminatory market does not require for its validation evidence that typists, working as typists and using the tools of the typing trade, could make deliveries of groceries to supermarkets.

What is required is that some modest number (certainly not all or even most) of the women who today are in the process of taking their first typically female jobs would have the ability and the willingness to take typically male jobs at the entry level, and that employers of workers in such jobs welcomed their entry and were committed to eliminating the harassment of women workers apparently so common in those jobs. If that modest number of women were willing to shift, as their current response to limited opportunities to make such a shift demonstrates is the case, then discrimination rather than women's choices is responsible for much of the wage gap between the sexes. The wage-setting process in the present market *is* tainted by discrimination. And it is that taint that invalidates the common assumption that market wages are sacrosanct.

MORE COMPLICATED CASES

The criterion developed to deal with realignment in the simple case presented above was that the realigned wages ought to have a pattern similar to that in a labor market in which sex discrimination was absent. In that example the recommended pattern—namely, equality in wages for the two occupations—also was the pattern that would have been chosen voluntarily by a nondiscriminating employer.

It is, I believe, enlightening, in dealing with more complicated cases in which there are many types of occupations and in which not everyone can do every job, to conduct a thought experiment. Suppose that one day all women were to disappear from the labor market, in the process vacating all the jobs they had held. Assume that for each woman who left, a man of identical talent and knowledge entered the labor market.

Some of the newly entered men would presumably be hired to replace the vanished women in previously female-type jobs. Others of them might go to work in male-type jobs for which they were competent. We can now ask what the occupational wage pattern might look like in the reconstituted labor market in which employers have been forced to give up sex discrimination by the disappearance of women on whom to practice it.

As a first approximation, each of the previously female-type occupations would assume the wage of the male-type occupation closest to it in terms of requirements of worker characteristics. Each such pair of jobs would have a common supply of labor, namely, all those who are competent to perform the pair of jobs and who are excluded by lack of competence from higher-wage jobs. A similar wage for any two paired jobs would make sense, exactly as in the simpler case in which there was only one pair of occupations. This first-order adjustment, which would raise the pay of jobs formerly held by women, would be a response to the difficulty of recruiting labor for those jobs at their old wage levels. The men who had replaced the women previously holding those jobs would have alternative options not available to women—in the paired jobs and in other previously all-male jobs requiring lower skills but paying higher wages than the previously female jobs. A pay raise would be required to retain those men in the previously female jobs.

As time went on, a second-order adjustment might be anticipated. We would expect that the numbers of workers whom managers would want to keep employed in the previously all-female jobs would decline because of the new necessity of paying them higher wages.

Both critics and advocates of comparable worth strategies have pointed to these disemployment effects as bolstering their arguments. Critics have argued that the resulting disemployment of women would more than cancel out the beneficial effects to women of higher wages. Advocates have argued that the disemployment effects would speed a beneficial desegregation of occupations, as the women disemployed from previously female-dominated occupations would be obliged to seek work in previously male-dominated fields. The experiment has been tried in Australia, where the actions of government-appointed boards with jurisdiction over occupational minimum wages resulted in large upward adjustments in average wages in female-dominated occupations. The Australian experience seems to suggest that disemployment effects need not be large (see Gregory and Duncan, 1981).

Even later, a third-order adjustment would occur, with a redefinition of the duties and requirements of particular jobs, as employers adjusted to the new wage pattern and rationalized their production processes to take account of it.

WAGE REALIGNMENT AND JOB EVALUATION

The realignment of wages in actual cases under the rubric of comparable worth would be the administered analogue to the first stage in the process of adjustment to a sex-blind labor market described in the last section. The second-order and third-order adjustments we have described could be expected to follow later through the operation of market forces rather than through administered changes.

In the discussion of the first-order adjustment process, the essential element is the grouping of jobs into sets that can draw labor from a common pool. The methodology of doing this in practice must surely have a great deal in common with job evaluation schemes in wide use in American business. These schemes describe jobs in terms of requirements for generalized abilities. Each job under consideration is assigned a numerical score for each kind of ability. The higher the quantity or quality of that ability the job is assumed to require, the higher is the corresponding score. The ability scores are then added up into a total score for each job. The reduction of a highly circumstantial job description to a single numerical score facilitates the comparison of jobs whose duties differ considerably in a qualitative way, in terms of the abilities required of the persons who fill them. Thus, the implementation of a job evaluation scheme in a comparable worth study takes the place of the pairing of male and female occupations in the illustrative discussion above. In principle, at any rate, the two procedures are quite similar.

This analysis has put emphasis on worker characteristics rather than on job characteristics. For at least some job evaluation schemes, the job characteristics included in the evaluation index have been chosen, consciously or unconsciously by the designers of these systems, because they imply the requirement for certain abilities in the incumbent worker. For example, the widely used Hay System awards scores for knowledge and problem-solving abilities required of and independence exercised by the worker.

Any particular scheme must be amended, before it is employed as a tool of analysis in a comparable worth case, to exclude sex bias in job evaluation. It is certainly doubtful that any existing scheme could be used without amendment in this way. As an example of obvious sexism, Hay System job evaluators were told to equate the skill necessary to operate a mimeograph machine (which requires about 10 minutes to learn) with the skill necessary to "operate a typewriter." Certainly a great deal of further research would be required before any particular job evaluation system could be endorsed for the purposes of wage realignment. However, we can have some confidence that an appropriately designed scheme, similar in principle to the job evaluation schemes currently in wide use in American business, could contribute to the achievement of a first-order approximation of the pattern that would emerge after discrimination had been ended.

CONCLUSION

This discussion has drawn the conclusion that the wage pattern in the existing segregation-ridden labor market is very different from the wage pattern that would be dictated by a market free of discriminatory sex segregation. The latter would be more efficient and more fair. An establishment-by-establishment realignment of wages with a pattern more congruent to a nondiscriminatory pattern would improve economic functioning in the long run.

The major challenge to economic research is that of building an economic model of the labor market for the purpose of estimating the pattern of wages that the free market would dictate in a nondiscriminatory world. One interesting question on which further research is needed is how close the existing or proposed job evaluation schemes come in terms of meeting the criterion of usefulness in this context—the ability to identify sets of jobs that can draw workers from a common labor supply, which would thus pay similar wages in a nondiscriminatory labor market.

A high-quality predictive model of wages in a labor market without discrimination would give validation to the claim that the wage realignments made using it would take account of comparable worth, as economists have traditionally understood worth to be measured, and would further pay equity.

REFERENCES

Bergmann, Barbara R.
  1971   The effect on white incomes of discrimination in employment. *Journal of Political Economy* (Fall).
Bergmann, Barbara R., and W. Darity
  1981   Social relations, productivity and employer discrimination. *Monthly Labor Review* (April).
Bergmann, Barbara R., and Mary Gray
  1984   The economics of compensation claims under Title VII. In Helen Remick, ed., *Comparable Worth and Salary Equity*. Philadelphia: Temple University Press.
Blau, Francine
  1976   *Equal Pay in the Office*. Lexington, Mass.: Lexington Books.
Gold, Michael Evans
  1983   *A Debate on Comparable Worth*. Ithaca, N.Y.: Industrial and Labor Relations Press.
Gregory, Robert G., and Ronald C. Duncan
  1981   The relevance of segmented labor market theories: The Australian experience of the achievement of equal pay for women. *Journal of Post Keynesian Economics* 3 (Spring):403-428.

The Economics of Comparable Worth: Analytical, Empirical, and Policy Questions

Mark R. Killingsworth

In this paper I present an economic analysis of the conceptual foundations of comparable worth and of its likely economic consequences, focusing on comparable worth as a remedy for sex discrimination.[1] The first section defines terms and describes the basic nature of comparable worth policy. The second section discusses the basic features of discriminatory labor markets, thereby describing the context within which proposed comparable worth policies would operate. The third section presents an economic analysis of the basic concepts underlying comparable worth, including in particular the notion that unequal pay for jobs of comparable worth is discriminatory. The final section examines the likely economic consequences of adopting and enforcing a comparable worth policy and contrasts comparable worth with alternative antidiscrimination policies.

WHAT IS COMPARABLE WORTH?

The first order of business in any discussion of comparable worth policy is to define clearly just what such a policy would entail. Three topics require special attention: comparability, coverage, and compliance.

---

[1] Technical details and formal demonstrations of the propositions developed heuristically in the text appear in a companion paper (M. Killingsworth, 1984b). For additional discussion, see my testimony before the Joint Economic Committee (M. Killingsworth, 1984a) and a related paper (M. Killingsworth, 1985).

Comparability

Many discussions of comparable worth (see Treiman and Hartmann, 1981:Ch. 4) provide a reasonably clear statement of the general nature of the standards that would be used to determine comparability: two jobs would be deemed comparable if they are found to require the same skill, effort, and responsibility and to involve the same working conditions. For example, to gauge skill requirements one might analyze the educational attainment and training of the persons in the two jobs in question; likewise, one might use formal job evaluations to derive measures of the effort and responsibility requirements and working conditions of the two jobs. The worth of any given job would then be computed as a weighted sum of the scores it receives for its working conditions and its skill, effort, and responsibility requirements. Two jobs would be deemed comparable if one job's worth, calculated in the manner just described, is the same as (or within a few points of) the other job's worth.

In a superficial sense, the job evaluations that would be used in determining the worth of different jobs would therefore be similar to those currently used by employers. However, there is one crucial difference between the kind of job evaluation that would be used with comparable worth policies and the kind of job evaluation typically used by employers: the latter are typically based explicitly on market considerations. For example, commercial job evaluation firms often benchmark wages for key jobs on the basis of labor market surveys and use procedures such as regression analysis of existing salary structures to determine the weights that the marketplace itself gives to the different factors considered (see Abowd, 1984; Schwab, 1980). In contrast, some analysts of comparable worth (e.g., Treiman and Hartmann, 1981:81–82) question such a market-oriented approach on the grounds that the wage relationships that currently exist are likely to be distorted by discrimination. Some comparable worth proponents advocate the use of bias-free job evaluations, i.e., ones that are derived independently of the existing wage structure and in which the weights given to the different factors considered (skill, effort, responsibility, and working conditions) would be determined on an a priori—or to put it less charitably, ad hoc—basis.

Implementing any procedure of this kind is likely to lead to lengthy and perhaps even bitter arguments over specifics (e.g., about the relative magnitudes that should be used in weighting the skill requirement and working condition components of any job's total worth). These are important questions of detail. However, a clear statement of the general principles that would be followed in determining comparability is sufficient for purposes of this analysis.

Coverage

Discussions of comparable worth usually do not specify clearly which jobs would be covered under a comparable worth requirement. In principle, the notion of comparable worth might be applied to literally all jobs, in which case coverage would be universal. In practice, however, most discussions of comparable worth present it as a remedy for sex discrimination. This suggests a simpler, partial rule: two jobs that are found to be comparable (in the sense defined above) would be required to pay the same wage only if women are a greater proportion of the workers in the low-paying job than in the high-paying job. (For example, see Blumrosen, 1979:496–497; Treiman and Hartmann, 1981:82–90; *Yale Law Journal*, 1981:677–678.)

Other questions about coverage have also been largely neglected. For example, would coverage be limited to employers with at least some specified number of employees, as under provisions of fair labor standards laws? Would the same comparable worth standard be applied to all establishments of a given employer, regardless of geographic location or industrial classification? Such details have not yet been discussed systematically.

One coverage question, however, does have an explicit answer. Contrary to the complaints of many critics who have charged that comparable worth would amount to government wage fixing on a national basis, most advocates of comparable worth have emphasized that comparable worth would be implemented on an employer-by-employer (or even an establishment-by-establishment) basis. Thus, although comparable worth might require a given employer to pay tool mechanics and secretaries the same wage (so long as the two jobs were found to be comparable at the firm in question), it would not establish a uniform national wage for secretaries (or tool mechanics) and would not necessarily require even that any other employer pay identical wages to tool mechanics and secretaries. That would depend on whether, at any other such firm, the jobs of tool mechanic and secretary were found to be comparable.

Compliance

Finally, most discussions of comparable worth are silent about compliance procedures, i.e., about how wages would be adjusted if two jobs covered by the comparable worth rule and deemed to be comparable are found to pay different wages. In principle, compliance could be achieved in an infinite variety of ways: the wage of the low-paying job could be raised to equal that of the high-paying job; or the wage of the high-paying job could be reduced to equal that of the low-paying job; or one could split the difference, raising the wage of the low-paying job and reducing the wage of the high-paying job until they are equal; and so forth. In practice, however, discussions of comparable worth that offer specifics on this question usually opt for wage increases in the low-paying job as either the only, or else the preferred, means of compliance.

Having defined the terms, I now proceed to substantive issues. I begin by describing the nature of discriminatory labor markets, by examining the context in which comparable worth strategies would operate. I then present an economic analysis of the conceptual foundations of comparable worth and of its likely economic effects.

EMPLOYER DISCRIMINATION: ANALYTICAL AND EMPIRICAL QUESTIONS

In order to understand the essential questions about discrimination underlying the comparable worth issue, it is useful to start by considering an imaginary economy with just two jobs, A and B. Employers' demands for workers to fill these two jobs depend on technology and on the demand for output. If the demand for output falls, employers' derived demands for workers in each job will likewise fall. If labor costs increase, the price of output will have to rise, thereby reducing the demand for output and, thus, in a roundabout way, reducing firms' derived demands for workers as well. Finally, if the wage in one job rises relative to the wage in the other job, then, even if the demand for output remains unchanged, employers will try to substitute away from the job whose wage has risen and toward the job whose wage has remained unchanged. Of course, particularly if the two jobs are quite different, the scope for such substitution may be quite limited.[2] (Much of the discussion below assumes that the scope for such substitution is small, though perhaps not completely nonexistent.)

In this imaginary economy, each individual worker is equally able to do either job equally well, but individuals are not all equally willing to do either job. In general, the supply of labor to the two jobs depends on both relative wages and individuals' preferences. At given wages, some individuals would prefer to do job A whereas others would prefer to do B. Indeed, persons with a particularly strong preference for B might want to do it even if the A wage was much higher than the B wage. Other individuals—those whose preference for B is weaker—could be induced to shift from B to A if the wage in A were to increase relative to the wage in B.[3] Thus, the higher the

---

[2] For example, it may be quite difficult to substitute the kind of work done by clerical workers for the kind of work done by craft workers (or vice versa) to any substantial degree. Likewise it may be quite difficult to substitute the kind of work done by nurses for the kind of work done by tree trimmers (or vice versa) to any substantial degree.

[3] Note that any shifting from B to A (or vice versa) that is stimulated by changes in relative wages might take a considerable time to work itself out; nothing in the discussion in the text assumes that such shifting would occur immediately.

A wage relative to the B wage, the greater the total supply of labor to job A—but even at very high relative wages, some workers would still prefer (want to work in) job B.

The actual relative wage (the wage in A relative to the wage in B) of course depends on demand as well as on supply. In general, there is no reason to expect that the two jobs would pay the same wage. For example, suppose that most workers regard job B as less attractive than job A and that, at the moment, both A and B pay the same wage. The number of workers who are willing to do job B may be too small to fill all the job B vacancies that employers want to fill at existing wage levels, and the number of workers who are willing to do job A may exceed the number of job A vacancies available. Under these conditions the B wage will tend to rise and the A wage will tend to fall. Eventually, B will pay more than A.

In this example, there is of course a pay differential—one job pays more than the other—but there need not be any sex differentials. If employers do not favor men over women in employment in either of the jobs, and if men's and women's preferences between the two jobs are not systematically different, then (1) the relative representation of women in the better-paid job, B, will be the same as the relative representation of women in the lower-paid job, A; and (2) men and women in the same job will receive the same pay.

Next, however, suppose that employers discriminate in favor of men in the sense that, at given wages, they would prefer to employ a man rather than a woman in the better-paid job B. In a situation of this kind, employers act as if men in job B produced not only actual output—steel, trimmed trees, and so on—but also provided an intangible that may be called maleness. This being the case, women will tend to be excluded from job B, and the women who are in job B will be paid less than the men in job B. Relative to a nondiscriminatory environment, employers' demands for male workers in job B are higher and their demands for female workers for job B are lower. Employment of women in job B is therefore lower and employment of men in job B is therefore higher than they would be in a nondiscriminatory world. The women who remain in job B will receive a lower wage than the men in job B (because the women do not produce maleness and so are less valuable to discriminatory employers than are men). Thus, there are now both pay differentials and sex differentials:

1. The women who are able to remain in job B are able to do so only because their wage falls below that of men in job B, meaning that the wage for women falls relative to the wage for men among B workers.

2. Discrimination in favor of men in job B acts to raise the B wage relative to the A wage among men.

3. The (relative) decline in the wage for women in job B, noted in item 1 above, means that the B wage falls relative to the A wage among women.

4. Women are now overrepresented in the low-paying job A and under-represented in the high-paying job B.

In evaluating these propositions it is important to clear away some of the confusion that plagues many discussions of discrimination. First, although it is often believed that discrimination is profitable for employers, discrimination will in fact reduce profits in the kind of labor market considered here. This is because a firm that employs a more expensive male worker in job B in preference to an equally productive but less expensive female worker is incurring greater costs than the minimum required to achieve a given level of production. (For elaboration of this point, see Ashenfelter and Pencavel, 1976.) In other words, if men and women are equally productive (as I have assumed) but nevertheless receive different wages in the same job, then an employer who is interested only in pecuniary profits will want his job B work force to consist entirely of women: otherwise, costs will be higher than the minimum possible. For example, when asked recently why most of the senior staff of his consulting firm is female, economist Alan Greenspan replied: "I always valued men and women equally, and I found that because others did not, good women economists were cheaper than men. Hiring women does two things: It gives us better quality work for less money, and it raises the market value of women."[4]

Ironically, some commentators stand this logic on its head and insist that employers cannot ignore "market realities." In their view, if employer X wants to hire a man, then employer X will have no choice but to match or exceed the offers made to that man by employers Y, Z, etc.—which quite possibly will exceed the offers made to equally productive women. (For a recent example of this argument, see Bodner, 1983.) Unfortunately, this appeal to market realities reveals a somewhat limited understanding of them: Why is it necessary to hire a higher-paid man, instead of a lower-paid but equally productive woman? For example, if the chairman of an academic department at a university hires or retains higher-salaried men in preference to lower-salaried but comparably productive women on the grounds that market realities have forced him or her to offer higher salaries to the men, then he or she is raising the department's costs but not its quality. The appropriate solution is that of Greenspan: to avoid hiring or retaining a higher-paid man, whenever it is possible to employ a comparably productive woman for less.

Finally, despite widespread assertions to the contrary, there is in fact no reason to believe that competition in the marketplace will eventually drive

---

[4] See Lewin (1983), who, oddly enough, refers to Greenspan's employment practices as "gender bias."

discriminatory employers out of business—even though, as just noted, such employers earn lower-than-normal profits.[5] As Goldberg (1982) has pointed out, even though discriminatory firms earn lower-than-normal pecuniary profits, they derive a kind of "psychic income," to the extent that they employ members of the group they prefer (e.g., men). Thus their total profits (meaning both pecuniary and psychic rewards for ownership) are more than sufficient to make them want to stay in business. Indeed, the monetary equivalent of the total profits of a discriminatory employer will exceed the pecuniary profits that could be earned by a nondiscriminatory employer using the same amount of capital. Thus, the greatest pecuniary payment that a nondiscriminatory employer would be willing to offer to take over the discriminatory employer's business is less than the minimum sum that the discriminatory employer would be willing to accept to sell the business. By the same token, because discriminatory firms earn lower pecuniary profits than nondiscriminatory firms, the maximum pecuniary payment that a discriminatory employer would be able to offer to take over the business of a nondiscriminatory employer is below the (pecuniary) profits earned by the nondiscriminatory employer. Thus, the nondiscriminatory employer would be unwilling to sell out to the discriminatory employer. In sum, even in a competitive economy, discriminatory and nondiscriminatory firms can coexist, even in the long run (see Goldberg, 1982, for details).

With these caveats in mind, now consider the four characteristics of discriminatory labor markets presented above. These are simply predictions about how the world would look in the presence of employer discrimination—predictions that, moreover, are derived from a very simple model of the economy. Is there any evidence to suggest that the real-world economy behaves in this way?

The available empirical evidence is certainly not conclusive, but it is suggestive. First, a number of studies have shown that there are indeed male-female pay differences within given jobs or job categories, as predicted by item 1 above, even when other things (e.g, personal, human capital, and job characteristics) are held constant (for examples of such studies, see Ashenfelter and Pencavel, 1976; O'Neill, 1983; Roos, 1981). Second, several empirical studies have found a strong negative association, other things being equal, between female representation and average pay (of men and women combined) within occupations, as predicted by item 4 above (see Treiman and Hartmann, 1981:Ch. 2, for a review of these stud-

---

[5] The notion that competition and discrimination are incompatible in the long run is dear to the hearts of both reactionaries (who believe that the economy is competitive and do not believe in the existence of discrimination) and radicals (who do not believe that the economy is competitive and do believe in the existence of discrimination).

ies). Finally, evidence in a number of studies suggests that, other things being equal, the reduction in pay associated with being in a mostly female occupation rather than in a mostly male occupation is greater for men than for women, as implied by items 2 and 3 above (for example, see O'Neill, 1983; Roos, 1981).

Inevitably, such studies are subject to methodological criticism, and further research on these issues is eminently desirable. (For discussion of some of the methodological defects in studies of this kind and suggestions for further research, see Bloom and Killingsworth, 1982.) Despite these caveats, however, it is noteworthy that the available evidence seems at least generally consistent with all four of the predictions derived from the model of discrimination presented here.

THE CONCEPTUAL BASIS OF COMPARABLE WORTH: AN ECONOMIC ANALYSIS

From the standpoint of economic analysis, the concept of comparable worth has two fundamental flaws. First, contrary to what many of its proponents assume, there is nothing inherently discriminatory in *unequal* pay for jobs of "comparable worth," and there is no reason why a nondiscriminatory labor market would necessarily entail *equal* pay for jobs of "comparable worth." Second, although proponents of comparable worth are correct in implicating employer discrimination as an important demand-side factor responsible for male-female pay differentials, they typically pay insufficient attention to the role of employee choices, which is an important supply-side factor that also contributes to such pay differentials.

Should Comparable Worth Necessarily Mean Equal Pay?

The first difficulty with comparable worth is its central premise: that unequal pay for jobs deemed to be of comparable worth is inherently discriminatory or, equivalently, that jobs deemed to be of comparable worth should receive the same wage. Unfortunately, this notion betrays a fundamental misunderstanding of the way in which labor markets (even nondiscriminatory ones) operate and of how employer discrimination harms women. *Unequal pay for jobs of comparable worth is not inherently discriminatory. Even in a sex-neutral labor market*—one in which sex is entirely irrelevant to market outcomes—*there is no reason why individuals in jobs of comparable worth should necessarily receive the same wage.*

The basic reason for this is simple. Individual tastes and preferences differ; comparability is in the eye of the beholder. Suppose that a given individual considers jobs A and B to be equally acceptable—i.e., would have no preference for one over the other if both jobs paid the same wage. Is there any reason to suppose that all other individuals would feel the same way? Would it be at all surprising if, at given wages, at least some individuals preferred A to B, while at the same time still other persons preferred B to A? Obviously not. Thus, even if the two jobs are found to be comparable according to a formal job evaluation scheme, there is no reason to suppose that all individuals will in fact view them as comparable. There is likewise no reason to suppose that supplies and demands for the two jobs would be equal if the two jobs paid the same wage. Hence, there is no reason to suppose that jobs that are comparable in the eyes of a given individual or job evaluation firm would in fact pay the same wage—even in a sex-neutral labor market.

The proponents and opponents of comparable worth have spent much time pondering whether it is possible to compare apples and oranges; the debate on this question, however, misses the essential point. On one hand, it is of course possible to compare apples and oranges (and secretaries and tool mechanics): we do it all the time, using the measuring rod of money. On the other hand, unless all individuals have exactly the same preferences, there is no substance to the notion that a nutritional evaluation of apples and oranges, or a job evaluation of secretarial and mechanic work, will have anything useful to say about the prices that these quantities could or should command in the marketplace.

For example, suppose apples and oranges do indeed have exactly the same nutritional content, and suppose further that all individuals are color-blind. Does it follow that apples and oranges will sell for the same price? Not unless all individuals regard apples and oranges as identical. Otherwise—if tastes are heterogeneous, so that some individuals like the taste of apples much better than that of oranges—the prices of apples and oranges will depend on both supply (e.g., production technology in the apple and orange industries) and demand factors (including the distribution or variation in individual tastes). In this case, it will be impossible to predict, a priori, whether apples will fetch a higher price than oranges (or vice versa), even if all individuals are color-blind (so that no one's behavior is influenced by the fact that oranges are usually orange-colored).

To many this point will be obvious.[6] Of course, individual tastes and

---

[6] But not, however, to Bergmann (in this volume). In her two-job model of the labor market, literally all suppliers of labor have identical preferences. That is, Bergmann tacitly assumes that, at equal wage rates, no one would prefer one job over another. This is the sole case in which one would indeed expect to observe equal pay for jobs of comparable worth in the absence of discrimination. However, in analytical terms it is a rather special case, offering little insight into the operation of real-world labor markets. In contrast, the model in this paper allows explicitly for the heterogeneity of tastes (see M. Killingsworth, 1984b, for details).

preferences differ, so perhaps some illustration may be worthwhile. Following is one example (from Sharon Smith: see Gold, 1983:43–44): an employer asks us to evaluate the comparability of the jobs of Spanish-English translator and French-English translator. A priori, it would seem difficult to argue that either of these two jobs requires more skill, effort, or responsibility than the other, and it would be surprising if, at a given firm, the working conditions for the two jobs were appreciably different. Presumably, then, most job evaluation schemes would conclude that these two jobs are comparable in terms of their working conditions and skill, effort, and responsibility requirements; and so, presumably, a comparable worth policy would require an employer to pay the same wage to persons in each of the two jobs.

But would pay for these two jobs necessarily be equal, even in a sex-neutral labor market? Perhaps, but now suppose we learn that the employer in question is located in Miami. Would it be reasonable to expect that Spanish-English translators in Miami would get the same pay as French-English translators in Miami? Almost certainly not. Would it even be possible to predict which job would receive the higher wage? Again, almost certainly not. True, one would expect that in Miami the supply of qualified Spanish-English translators would be greater than the supply of qualified French-English translators. Other things being equal, that would mean that the latter job would pay more than the former. However, other things are not necessarily equal, even in a sex-neutral labor market. In particular, Miami's demand for Spanish-English translators might well be greater than its demand for French-English translators. Other things being equal, that would mean that the latter job would pay less than the former.[7]

As this example indicates, even in a labor market in which sex is irrelevant, wages are determined by market supplies and demands rather than by comparability—which may have little or nothing to do with wage determination. The reason is that supplies and demands summarize the tastes and preferences of all individuals, whereas comparability merely indicates the tastes and preferences of one individual or of a single entity (e.g., a job evaluation firm). Whether the individual who determines comparability is *l'homme moyen sensuel* (or *la femme moyenne sensuelle*) is beside the point:

---

[7] A difficulty with the translators example is that one must assume that the two translation jobs would in fact be found comparable. Although plausible, this assumption is still only an assumption. However, the real world provides illustrations of the same point. For example, Gold (1983:48–49) reports the results of a 1976 job evaluation undertaken for the state of Washington. The job of park ranger received 181 evaluation points, whereas the job of homemaker received 182 evaluation points. Is there any reason to believe that these two supposedly comparable jobs would necessarily receive the same pay, even if sex were altogether irrelevant to all labor market outcomes?

most distributions have observations on either side of the median, and market demands and supplies depend on those observations as well as on the median. Note that this result holds whether or not demand is affected by employer discrimination: it is just as pertinent in a discriminatory as in a nondiscriminatory labor market.

In sum, comparable jobs need not receive the same wage. Similarly, there is no reason to believe that noncomparable jobs would necessarily receive different wages. An example of this derives from Adam Smith (1776). In discussing wage differentials among jobs, Adam Smith expressed his view that the butcher's trade is a "brutal and odious business" and noted that it paid more than other trades with similar skill requirements. As modern writers have observed, however, this may have been due to the cultural homogeneity of eighteenth-century Britain (i.e., essentially identical preferences for all individuals). A pay differential between butchering and other trades need not arise, despite the supposedly brutal and odious nature of butchers' work, if preferences are heterogeneous. As Rees (1976:340) has pointed out, if enough individuals have no strong feelings about or actually enjoy butchering, "it would then clearly be possible to fill all positions for butchers without any compensating wage differential."

Similarly, consider police work. Police work is generally regarded as arduous and dangerous, and it would hardly be surprising if, in recognition of this, a job evaluation were to award more job evaluation points to police work than to clerical work. Under a comparable worth standard, then, police work might well be entitled to a higher rate of pay than many kinds of clerical work. But would such a pay differential really be necessary? If enough individuals think of police work as exciting and regard clerical work as dull, it would be possible to fill all police jobs without paying any wage premium at all. (Nor is this merely a hypothetical possibility: consider the lengthy waiting lists of qualified applicants seeking positions in many municipal police departments around the country.) In such a case comparable worth would serve to justify and protect the practice of paying premium wages for police work—a job still held mostly by men—despite the absence of any rational basis for such a differential.

The reasoning in the police and butchers examples is essentially the same as the reasoning in the translators case: statements about the comparability or noncomparability of jobs are simply expressions of a given individual's or job evaluation firm's feelings about those jobs; wages, however, depend on supplies and demands, i.e., on all individuals' tastes and preferences. Job evaluation points will accurately reflect all individuals' tastes and preferences among jobs only if all individuals have identical tastes and preferences. In that case, a priori (or bias-free) job evaluations of the kind envisaged by advocates of comparable worth will indeed provide a useful guide to wage differentials among jobs. Otherwise, however, such evaluations may provide little or no meaningful information about market supplies to or wage differentials among jobs.[8]   When tastes are heterogeneous, jobs do not have any intrinsic absolute worth; indeed, they do not even have any intrinsic relative worth. According to one proponent of comparable worth, "The comparable worth strategy seeks to adjust market wages, via job evaluation, to where they would be in the absence of discrimination" (Hartmann, 1984:21). Although that may well be the objective of comparable worth advocates, it is simply wishful thinking to imagine that job evaluation can in fact determine what the wage structure would be in the absence of discrimination.

What If Labor Supply Is Sex-Related?

The arguments just presented are sufficient to dispose of a strict comparable worth policy of requiring equal pay for comparable jobs. However, it does not dispose of the basic problem—sex discrimination—that is a major motivation for most proposals for comparable worth. In particular, although there is no reason why comparable jobs would pay the same wages if sex were irrelevant to labor market outcomes, there is also no reason why a sex-neutral labor market would exhibit the negative empirical association, noted at the outset, between overall average pay and the proportion female in different jobs. Indeed, if the labor market were truly sex-neutral, then, even though one would not expect to find equal pay for jobs deemed to be of comparable worth, one would expect to find the same male-female employment ratio in all jobs, other things (skills and so forth) being equal.

---

[8] The skeptic may ask: If the usefulness of job evaluations is limited or nonexistent, why do firms undertake them? One important reason has to do with a basic difference (noted above) between the bias-free job evaluations advocated by comparable worth proponents and the market-oriented evaluations typically used by firms. Bias-free evaluations would be undertaken on an a priori basis without reference to marketplace supplies and demands. In contrast, the market-oriented job evaluations usually used by employers are in general based squarely on market considerations (e.g., benchmarking wages for key jobs on the basis of wage surveys). As such, market-oriented job evaluations may be regarded as attempts to gauge the shortages or surpluses that would develop if wages were set only on the basis of skill, effort, responsibility, and working conditions (as in a bias-free job evaluation), and to adjust wages accordingly. It should be noted that there is nothing inherently sacred about the concept of wage determination by forces of supply and demand. (For example, as emphasized above, employer discrimination—a force that affects demand—will certainly distort wages and wage differentials among jobs.) However, establishing the existence of employer discrimination does not establish the validity of the concept of comparable worth, and establishing the existence of unequal pay for jobs of comparable worth is not sufficient to establish the existence of employer discrimination. Indeed, as noted earlier in this section, there is no reason to expect equal pay for jobs of comparable worth even in a completely nondiscriminatory labor market, which is presumably the ideal or reference point that most comparable worth advocates would adopt.

Thus, even though job comparability and a strict comparable worth policy have no basis in analysis or logic, one might still argue for a modified comparable worth policy. Under such a policy, which I will call CW-1 for short, employers would be required to pay the same wage to workers in two jobs that are found to be comparable if (but only if) women are a greater proportion of the workers in the lower-paying job than in the higher-paying job (for example, see Blumrosen, 1979). More generally, under CW-1, the concept of comparable worth might be redefined as requiring only that wages in different jobs be equal to what they would be if gender were truly irrelevant to labor market behavior. Thus, CW-1 would not necessarily require equal pay for jobs of comparable worth (because it would leave undisturbed any pay differences among comparable jobs to the extent that such differences would occur in a sex-neutral labor market). It would, however, be concerned with sex-related pay differences among jobs—which are a major motivation for much of the discussion of comparable worth. It might be quite difficult, in practice, to determine the pay rates in different jobs that would obtain if sex as such were irrelevant to labor market outcomes. Leaving such questions of practicality aside, however, what can one say about the merits of such a modified comparable worth policy?

Like a strict policy of requiring equal pay for jobs of comparable worth, CW-1 is open to serious question. Contrary to what many proponents of comparable worth appear to assume, the wage structure that would prevail if sex were irrelevant to all labor market activity is not necessarily the same as the wage structure that would prevail in the absence of employer discrimination. In the real-world labor market, decisions of workers (labor supply) as well as decisions of employers (labor demand) are sex-related. Even if sex did not affect labor demand (i.e., even if employers did not discriminate), sex differences in labor supply decisions—in preferences among jobs— would still lead to pay differences among jobs, even jobs of comparable worth.

To see this, return to the simple two-job economy described above. In that discussion I implicitly assumed that there was no systematic sex difference in job preferences—i.e., that at any given set of wage rates the proportion of women who desire to do either job is the same as the proportion of men. In that case, in the absence of employer discrimination, both jobs would have the same sex composition: the male:female employment ratios in both jobs would be the same. Now suppose instead, however, that women prefer job A to a greater extent than do men in the sense that, at any given set of wage rates, the proportion of women who desire to do job A exceeds the proportion of men. In this case the total supply of labor to job A will be greater and the total supply of labor to job B smaller than if women's preferences for A were the same (on average) as those of men. Relative to a setting in which women's average job preferences are the same as those of men, the wage in job A relative to that in job B will therefore be lower; and women will be overrepresented in job A (i.e., the male:female employment ratio will be higher in job B than in job A).

Some proponents of comparable worth recognize that overrepresentation of women in some jobs and wage differentials among jobs may to some extent be a consequence of women's own choices rather than of employer discrimination. The National Research Council (NRC) report on comparable worth (Treiman and Hartmann, 1981:53)—which, it should be noted, endorsed the general concept—provides an admirable summary of many of the reasons why women may be overrepresented in low-wage jobs:

First, women may be socialized to believe that some types of jobs are appropriate and that others are inappropriate for women; socialization may be so effective for some women that it never even occurs to them to consider other types of jobs. Second, women may have pursued courses of study they thought particularly appropriate to women and in consequence may not have the education or training that would suit them for other available jobs. Third, women may lack information about other available jobs, their pay rates, working conditions, and access to them. Fourth, women may be aware of alternatives, but because of actual or expected family obligations may structure their labor force participation in particular ways [that reduce their earnings possibilities]. For example, they may be unwilling to invest a great deal of time, effort, or money in preparing for jobs because they do not expect to remain in the labor force after marriage or after childbearing. . . . Fifth, women may be aware of alternative types of jobs but believe them to be unavailable or unpleasant because of discrimination; their labor market preparation and behavior may be affected in many ways by this perception: the course of study they take; the time, money, and effort invested in training; their willingness to accept promotion, etc.

Many of these factors might well be cited as forms of societal discrimination; only one of them can readily be characterized as a form of clear-cut employer discrimination. Perhaps most important, factors such as these suggest that choices made prior to labor market entry, as distinct from employer discrimination, can have an important effect on sex differences in labor market outcomes. For example, Polachek (1978) investigated the college majors of young men and women. As one might expect, his data showed considerable gender differences in college majors: business and engineering were particularly popular among the young men; education, home economics, and medically related fields such as nursing were particularly popular among the young women. What is striking and rather unexpected is that these differences persist even after statistical adjustment for such factors as Scholastic Aptitude Test (SAT) verbal and mathematical scores and a set of attitudinal variables (measuring such things as individuals' assessments of the lifetime importance, to them, of steady work,

money, and friends). That is, young men and young women tend to choose different college majors even when other things (abilities and attitudes) are the same.

A second example of the same idea derives from *Lemons* v. *City and County of Denver* (620 F.2d 228 [10th Cir.] cert. denied, 449 U.S. 888 [1980]), a comparable worth case in which nurses maintained that their predominantly female job paid less than predominantly male jobs (e.g., gardener-florist or tree trimmer) that were allegedly comparable to the job of nurse. Although the nurses maintained that Denver was discriminating against them, they did not allege that Denver had excluded them from the comparable but higher-paid and predominantly male jobs. Indeed, asked if she had ever considered switching from nursing to tree trimming, one of the *Lemons* plaintiffs said: "I wouldn't work purely for money, not outside nursing. That's what I like to do" (see V. Killingsworth, 1981:17).

In the examples of choice of college major and nursing, the basic point is the same: individual choice as well as (or instead of) employer discrimination can lead to a concentration of women in low-wage jobs. The consequences of this for comparable worth policies are rarely appreciated, however. Two implications are particularly important for evaluation of proposals for comparable worth.

The first is that systematic differences in sex preferences rather than employer discrimination may account for at least some of the negative empirical association, noted above, between overall average pay (for both sexes combined) and the proportion female in different jobs. In other words, employer discrimination of the kind discussed above will lead to overrepresentation of women in low-paying jobs, but evidence of overrepresentation of women in low-paying jobs does not necessarily constitute evidence of employer discrimination. It may instead simply be evidence of systematic sex differences in job preferences, as in the example just discussed.

Second, and more generally, the wage structure that would obtain in the absence of employer discrimination is not necessarily the same as the wage structure that would obtain if sex were entirely irrelevant to labor market behavior (meaning both supply and demand). The two wage structures would be identical only if sex were irrelevant to labor supply as well as labor demand. This is ignored by both a strict comparable worth policy (which would require equal pay for jobs of comparable worth) and CW-1 (which would require only that workers be paid what they would receive if sex as such were irrelevant to labor market outcomes, even if that meant wage differentials among jobs deemed to be of comparable worth). In other words, neither kind of policy recognizes the possibility that even in the absence of employer discrimination sex differences in preferences and

therefore in labor supply decisions might lead to a concentration of women in low-paid jobs (e.g., nursing or secretarial work).[9]

ECONOMIC CONSEQUENCES OF COMPARABLE WORTH AND OTHER REMEDIES FOR DISCRIMINATION

Whatever the merits or defects of the conceptual basis for comparable worth, to many the most important question about comparable worth has to do with whether it would be a suitable remedy for discrimination. This section compares comparable worth and other antidiscrimination measures and evaluates the consequences of each.

Economic Consequences of Comparable Worth

To sum up the argument so far:

1. There is no reason why jobs of comparable worth would or should necessarily receive the same wage, even in a labor market in which sex is irrelevant.

2. To the extent that job preferences (i.e., labor supply decisions) are sex-related, it is entirely possible that one would find women concentrated in low-paying jobs even in the absence of employer discrimination (i.e., even if sex were irrelevant to labor demand decisions).

3. There is therefore little or no justification for comparable worth, at least as usually defined. When job comparability provides little or no useful information about the wage structure that would prevail in a labor market in which sex is entirely irrelevant, there is no merit in requiring equal pay for jobs of comparable worth. Moreover, when job preferences are sex-related, there is little merit in a modified comparable worth policy that would, in effect, set wages without reference to such sex differences in job preferences.

It should be emphasized immediately that none of this means either (1) that employers do not discriminate on the basis of sex or (2) that employer discrimination does not lead to overrepresentation of women in low-paying

---

[9] Reasoning similar to that given in the text leads to parallel conclusions about the effect of a systematic preference for job B on the part of men: other things being equal, the job B wage would fall relative to the job A wage, and men would be overrepresented in job B. On balance, then, women's average preference for job A would have to be stronger than men's average preference for job B if the net effect of these sex differences were to lead to a differential favoring job B and to overrepresentation of women in job A.

jobs. Indeed, if sex differences in job preferences were the only reason why women are concentrated in low-paying jobs, one would expect to find that men and women earn the same wage within given jobs—but the available evidence indicates that that is not the case.

This suggests that there might still be some scope for comparable worth, albeit in still more modified form. Under this (further) modification of comparable worth policy, which I will call CW-2, employers would in principle be required to adjust pay in different jobs so as to yield the wage structure that would be observed in the absence of employer discrimination against women. Determining what this wage structure would look like would obviously be difficult. Thus, in practice, CW-2 would probably amount to something much simpler and more straightforward: a policy of requiring wage increases for jobs in which women are overrepresented (for example, see Clauss, 1981:85; *Yale Law Journal*, 1981:680).

As implied already, the pay adjustments that would ideally be required under CW-2 would almost certainly differ from the changes that would generate the wage structure that would prevail if sex were irrelevant to both labor demand and labor supply decisions. In addition, the pay adjustments required under the ideal CW-2 policy would almost certainly not require equality of pay rates among jobs judged to be comparable in terms of a formal job evaluation. Nevertheless, CW-2 would directly confront one of the most important consequences of employer discrimination: low pay for women. Thus, CW-2 in its ideal form would certainly address a central concern of most proponents of comparable worth, even though it would have little or nothing to do with the comparability of different jobs.

Moreover, in practice, CW-2 as it would actually be implemented has appeal even for those who, on principle, would prefer CW-1. First, it could be argued that sex differences in job preferences are essentially a result of sex discrimination. True, the discrimination that induces girls to consider nursing or teaching as appropriate work and to consider tree trimming or tool mechanics as inappropriate is societal discrimination rather than employer discrimination in the usual sense. However, in this view, the means through which such discrimination is practiced are of secondary importance; what is crucial is the fact that it is, after all, discrimination. Requiring employers to raise wages for low-paying, predominantly female jobs does not attack the source of this discrimination, but it does at least attack some of its effects (Gold, 1983:94-95).

A second justification for simply requiring wage increases in female-dominated, low-wage jobs (CW-2, in practice) is that alternatives to such a policy are unsatisfactory. The conventional approach to employer discrimination as such is to break down discriminatory barriers that keep women out of high-paid jobs and to require equal pay for equal work. Eventually such measures will completely counteract the effects of employer discrimination: women's relative representation in high-paying jobs will rise, and sex differentials within the same job will be erased (for example, see Johnson and Welch, 1976). However, the full impact of such measures may not be felt for some time to come (*Yale Law Journal*, 1981:680).[10]

Moreover, in this view, conventional antidiscrimination measures cannot realistically be expected to do much for older cohorts of women workers; these women entered low-paying jobs some years ago (either because societal discrimination induced them to choose such jobs or because employer discrimination prevented them from entering other jobs), and they are now locked in. Providing access to high-paying jobs can do little for such women; they do not have the training required for such jobs (and at midcareer it usually makes little sense to get such training), and now, if only because of their initial socialization and the development of habits over time, such women might not even want to be in other jobs, despite the higher pay. A policy of requiring wage increases for predominantly female, low-paying jobs would provide immediate benefits for such women—who, in this view, have little to gain from conventional antidiscrimination measures (see Blumrosen, 1979:491–492; Clauss, 1981:81, 91–92; Treiman and Hartmann, 1981:66–67).

Unfortunately, requiring wage increases for predominantly female low-paying jobs is likely to have serious, albeit unintended, adverse side effects, not merely for women as a whole but for older cohorts of women workers in particular.

To see why, return to the simple two-job economy discussed above and consider the effects of a wage increase for the predominantly female low-wage job, A, in the short run, i.e., when supplies of labor to the two jobs are essentially fixed. This case is particularly relevant to understanding the effect of comparable worth on older cohorts of women workers, who are locked into job A (in the sense that they could not easily switch to job B and might not even want to do so).

The benefits of increasing the wage for job A are obvious: the A wage will rise both in absolute terms and, of perhaps equal significance, relative to wages (of both men and women)[11] in the high-paying job B. In other words,

---

[10] Although the available evidence is certainly not conclusive, recent research suggests that—contrary to what many proponents of comparable worth appear to believe—conventional antidiscrimination measures have increased the female:male earnings ratio, female representation in previously predominantly male jobs, and so on (see Beller, 1978, 1980, 1982; Brown, 1982; Leonard, 1984a, 1984b).

[11] Recall that when employers discriminate, women in job B will be paid less than men in job B. Thus, there are really two job B wages, not one.

not only will the modified comparable worth policy raise wages in low-wage jobs, it will also narrow the pay gap between low-wage and high-wage jobs.

In addition to these benefits, however, the policy also has costs. Although they are perhaps less obvious than its benefits, they are no less significant. It is particularly important to note that comparable worth imposes costs not only on employers but also on women (and men) in low-wage, predominantly female jobs—the very group the policy is intended to help.

First, since the A wage rises, firms' demands for A workers will fall, leading to unemployment for some workers now in job A—who are disproportionately female. Second, the increase in the A wage raises labor costs and therefore prices, so consumer demand will fall. As consumer demand falls, employers' output will contract, leading to decreases in the demand for job B (and thus to decreases in the demands for both male and female workers in job B).[12] In turn, the decline in the demand for job B will lead to unemployment and/or lower wages for both men and women initially in job B. In particular, the wage of women in job B will fall by more than the wage of men in job B, thereby widening the sex differential in pay in job B.[13]

In sum, increasing the A wage in accordance with a modified comparable worth policy will obviously raise the A wage and reduce the differential between the A wage and the B wage (of either men or women). However, the policy will also have some unfortunate side effects:

1. The number of workers in job A will fall and unemployment of workers formerly in job A will rise.
2. Wages for both men and women in job B will fall.
3. The wage differential between men and women in job B will widen.
4. Employment and output will fall and consumer prices will rise.

Thus, in the short run, some women (and men) workers in job A will gain, but everyone else—all men and all women in job B and all other women (and men) in job A—will lose. The notion that raising wages in low-paid, predominantly female jobs will help older cohorts of women who are locked into those jobs is at best half true: such a policy will certainly benefit some of these women but, by reducing the total demand for such jobs, will necessarily harm the rest of them.

Now consider the effects of increasing the wage in job A in the long run,

---

[12] This decrease in demand for workers to fill job B will be offset by an increase in the demand for such workers, to the extent that it is possible to substitute job B for job A. In the nature of the case, however, the scope for such substitution is likely to be rather small; see n. 2 above.

[13] In intuitive terms, this is because the comparable worth policy forces an increase in the A wage, so that the portion of the discrimination against women that used to show up as a reduced A wage will now show up as a wider male-female differential within job B.

i.e., allow for the fact that, given sufficient time, supplies of labor to the two jobs will adjust to the changed wages prevailing for those jobs. As in the short-run case, the comparable worth policy will raise the A wage both absolutely and relative to the B wage (of men or women).[14] Again, then, the comparable worth policy raises wages in the low-wage, predominantly female jobs and narrows the pay gap between low-wage and high-wage jobs.

However, in the long run as in the short-run, the policy of raising pay for job A will also have several adverse side effects. First, as in the short-run case, firms' demands for workers for job A will fall as the A wage rises. This will reduce employment of workers in job A, leading to unemployment for some individuals who would otherwise be in job A. (Since women are overrepresented in job A, this unemployment will hit women harder than men.) Second, the increase in the A wage relative to the wage for both men and women in job B attracts workers toward job A and away from job B.[15] This reduces employment of both men and women in job B. In the absence of any restraint on the A wage, this increase in the supply of labor to job A would drive the A wage back to its original level. However, the comparable worth policy prevents the A wage from falling; instead, the increased supply to job A turns into more unemployment. Finally, since total employment in job A declines and employment of both men and women in job B also declines, production drops. The drop in production results in an increase in the price level.

Are these predictions about the effects of comparable worth policies supported by any empirical evidence?

The United States has not implemented comparable worth strategies to any considerable extent, but Australia's experience with its policy of enforcing equal pay for work of equal value is illuminating. Under the policy,

---

[14] Thus, the policy-induced increase in the A wage will necessarily reduce the B wage of both men and women relative to the A wage. However, it is not possible to be certain about the impact of the increase in the A wage on the levels of the B wage for either men or women. On one hand, as in the short-run case, the increase in the A wage raises labor costs and thus prices. Other things being equal, this will reduce firms' demands for job B and will therefore reduce B wages for both men and women. On the other hand, in the long run (but not in the short run), the rise in the A wage relative to the B wage (for both men and women) attracts labor away from job B and toward job A (see text below). Other things being equal, this will reduce the supplies of both men and women to job B and will therefore raise the B wage (of both men and women). The net impact of these two forces on wages in job B is indeterminate a priori: it depends on whether the supply effects are greater or less than the demand effects. All one can say for sure is that B wages for both men and women will fall or, if they rise, will rise by a smaller proportion than the A wage.

[15] That is, some workers now in job B will try to switch to job A, and some individuals who are now choosing a job will drop any plans they might have made to train for job B and will seek training for and employment in job A instead.

which began in 1972, Australia's federal and state wage tribunals have set the same rate of pay (regardless of the gender of the majority of incumbents) for all jobs judged to be comparable in terms of skill, effort, responsibility, and working conditions. The tribunals fix minimum rates (not actual levels) of pay and have considerable latitude in determining comparability (Gregory and Duncan, 1981:408). These potential loopholes notwithstanding, Australia's comparable worth policy apparently had a substantial effect on the aggregate female:male earnings ratio: that ratio (for full-time nonmanagerial adult workers in the private sector) rose from .607 in 1971 to .766 in 1977 (Gregory and Duncan, 1981:409).

For purposes of this discussion, however, the most interesting aspect of Australia's experience is that the policy's side effects appear to have been generally adverse. Gregory and Duncan (1981:418) found that increases in women's wages attributable to the policy reduced the rate of growth of female employment (below the rate that would otherwise have prevailed), relative to the rate of growth of men's employment, in (1) manufacturing, (2) services, and (3) overall (i.e., in all industries combined). Comparable worth had a negligible effect on the relative employment growth rate of women only in the public authority and community services sector. Their overall estimates imply that, as of 1977, the cumulative effects of the policy served to reduce the rate of growth of women's employment, relative to that of men, by almost one-third.

Moreover, these estimates may understate the actual effect of the comparable worth policy. First, among the things Gregory and Duncan controlled for in deriving their results was the male unemployment rate (which, as indicated above, may also be affected by comparable worth policies). Second, due to data limitations, Gregory and Duncan analyzed the impact of comparable worth on the growth in the number of women employed without reference to its effect on the hours worked by women workers. Recent research suggests that the impact of comparable worth on hours worked was also negative and that focusing solely on numbers of employed women may therefore understate the full effect of the comparable worth policy on employment opportunities for women (Gregory and Duncan, 1983; McGavin, 1983a,b; Snape, 1980).

Gregory and Duncan also analyzed the impact of the policy on female joblessness. Their estimates imply that the policy's cumulative impact as of 1977 was an increase in the female unemployment rate of about 0.5 of a percentage point. (The actual female unemployment rate in August 1976 was 6.2 percent.)

In sum, the Gregory and Duncan study indicates that Australia's "equal pay for work of equal value" policy adversely affected both the rate of relative employment growth for women and the female unemployment rate, as implied by the analysis in this section.[16]

The Gregory and Duncan findings that Australia's comparable worth policy had no appreciable effect on women's relative employment in the public authority and community service sector highlight two potential exceptions to the general propositions presented above: the government sector and nursing.

Much of the impetus for comparable worth seems to have come from public-sector employees, notably the American Federation of State, County, and Municipal Employees (AFSCME) (see Bureau of National Affairs, 1981). This may well be no accident. In contrast with the private sector, the government sector will have little or no difficulty (at least in the short run) in maintaining the demand for its "output" at existing levels, despite policy-induced increases in its labor costs. To cover the increased labor costs, government can simply compel the rest of the economy to pay higher taxes, keeping its real revenues unchanged. (The private sector will try to cover policy-induced increases in labor costs by raising its prices, but it cannot compel the rest of the economy to go on purchasing the same amount of its output at the higher prices.)

At least in the short run, then, declining demand for public-sector output (and thus declining derived demand for public-sector workers) is not likely

---

[16] Without implying that they necessarily share the opinions expressed in this paper, I would like to thank both Gregory and Duncan for several very helpful discussions of the findings and implications of their study. It is worth noting that numerous advocates of comparable worth in the United States are under the erroneous impression that the Gregory-Duncan study shows that comparable worth had little or no adverse effect on women's employment growth or unemployment rate (for details, see M. Killingsworth, 1984a). The reason for this seems to be that Gregory and Duncan presented two kinds of results: a set of simple descriptive statistics showing the raw or unadjusted time series of women's relative employment growth and relative unemployment rates and a set of regression analyses aimed at isolating the effect of comparable worth, other things being equal, on these measures of women's economic status. The simple time series show that relative employment grew and the relative unemployment rate fell, both before and after introduction of comparable worth. This is apparently the basis of claims by comparable worth advocates in the United States that Australia's policy had no adverse effects. However, by their nature, simple time series data do not abstract from changes in employment or unemployment rates that are attributable to forces other than comparable worth. In contrast, the regression results presented by Gregory and Duncan and discussed in the text explicitly abstract from changes in employment or unemployment rates attributable to forces other than comparable worth (e.g., business cycle fluctuations and secular trends). As noted in the text, those results indicate that, other things being equal, the comparable worth policy reduced women's relative employment growth and raised women's unemployment rate. In other words, the results indicate that, if other factors had remained the same, women's relative employment growth would have been greater and the women's unemployment rate would have been lower had Australia not adopted comparable worth.

to be substantial. However, as experience with Proposition 13 indicates, whether this will be equally true in the long run is an open question. Note also that the absence of an appreciable short-run effect on women's relative employment in the government sector has nothing to do with the reasons for, or the extent of, the policy-induced increases in wages for mainly female jobs in that sector. That is, the short-run effects of the policy would be negligible regardless of whether wages in such jobs are raised to a level that is (still) below, equal to, or in excess of wages in "comparable," predominantly male jobs.

Nursing is another possible exception to the generally gloomy outlook regarding the likely effects of comparable worth (and it may well be no accident that nurses, like public employees, have been in the forefront of agitation for comparable worth; see Bureau of National Affairs, 1981). However, as I will explain shortly, the reasons may have little or nothing to do with the alleged comparability of nursing and predominantly male jobs.

Alternatives to Comparable Worth

Rejecting comparable worth certainly does not dispose of the problems of discrimination that have motivated many of the proponents of comparable worth. If comparable worth is not the answer to these problems, what is? This section considers two alternatives: conventional antidiscrimination measures (e.g., equal pay and equal access provisions of Title VII of the Civil Rights Act) and novel expansion or application of antitrust laws.

Conventional Antidiscrimination Measures

The essential difference between comparable worth and conventional antidiscrimination measures is very simple. Conventional antidiscrimination measures make it costly for employers to treat equally qualified men and women differently. Comparable worth makes it costly for employers to employ low-wage, predominantly female labor. As shown above, comparable worth solves the problem of the artificially wide gap between low-wage, predominantly female jobs and high-wage, predominantly male jobs only to create other problems, including, in particular, reduced opportunities for women in both low-wage and high-wage jobs. In contrast, conventional antidiscrimination measures compel discriminatory employers to provide greater opportunities for women workers (by making it costly for such employers to deny equal pay or equal access to women with the same skills and qualifications as men).

To the extent that conventional antidiscrimination measures are actually implemented, the wages of women rise for three distinct reasons. Two of these are obvious. Equal pay requirements raise the wages of women within given jobs, and equal access requirements make it possible for qualified women to switch from low-wage to high-wage jobs. A third reason is more subtle: to the extent that wages respond to changes in supplies and demands (a matter to which I will return presently), the fact that some women are able to leave low-wage jobs for high-wage jobs will reduce supply to the low-wage jobs, leading to wage increases for low-wage jobs.

Nor do conventional antidiscrimination measures lead to the kinds of adverse side effects that are fostered by comparable worth. True, each type of antidiscrimination remedy makes certain forms of behavior more costly. But, whereas comparable worth makes it more costly to employ low-wage, predominantly female labor, conventional antidiscrimination measures make it more costly to treat equally qualified men and women differently. In particular, such measures in effect force employers to incur costs (e.g., back pay) whenever they do not treat equally qualified men and women as equals. Depending on how stringent these requirements are and how vigorously they are enforced, the pecuniary costs they impose on employers will offset the nonpecuniary or intangible factor of maleness that makes discriminatory employers want to treat equally qualified men and women differently. In consequence, stringent conventional antidiscrimination measures, stringently applied, will reverse all the effects of employer discrimination described earlier (Johnson and Welch, 1976).

To be sure, some comparable worth proponents see comparable worth as a complement to, not a substitute for, conventional antidiscrimination measures such as Title VII. Their reasoning seems to be as follows: conventional antidiscrimination measures will indeed eventually raise wages and employment of women to the levels that would prevail in the absence of discrimination. However, such measures have worked (and will continue to work) very slowly. Comparable worth offers the prospect of substantial and rapid increases in pay, bringing women's wages much more quickly to the levels that would prevail in the absence of discrimination. To the extent that it leads to wage increases, comparable worth will certainly also mean reductions in women's employment. However, such job losses will eventually be overcome as conventional antidiscrimination measures continue to open up job opportunities for women. In sum, conventional antidiscrimination measures will ultimately move the labor market to nondiscriminatory employment and wage levels for women whether or not comparable worth is adopted. However, introducing comparable worth will provide many women with nondiscriminatory wage levels much more quickly than would be the case if comparable worth is not added to conventional antidiscrimination measures.

Unfortunately, the premises underlying this reasoning are shaky. In effect, comparable worth asks women to choose between (1) immediate wage increases and accompanying immediate employment reductions via comparable worth, followed by eventual employment increases (attained via conventional measures exclusively)—the comparable worth strategy—and (2) slower but steadier gains in both wages and employment via conventional measures alone. It is not obvious that (1) is the better of the two alternatives. Second, as noted earlier, job evaluation cannot be expected to identify the wage structure that would exist in the absence of discrimination; the wage increases that would be required under comparable worth would be quite unlikely to be the same as the wage changes that would bring about a nondiscriminatory wage structure. Partly because of this, comparable worth is likely to be resisted not only by discriminatory employers but also (and with good reason) by truly nondiscriminatory firms. Thus, the notion that comparable worth may provide quick wage increases may be seriously mistaken; if anything, employer resistance to comparable worth will be stronger than employer resistance to conventional antidiscrimination measures. Finally, comparable worth diverts resources and energy that could otherwise have been devoted to implementation of conventional measures. That is particularly ironic because, once the adverse employment effects of comparable worth take place, a redoubling of conventional antidiscrimination efforts will be necessary to counteract them.

Antitrust Laws and the Problem of Employer Cartels

As noted earlier, conventional antidiscrimination measures can be expected to raise pay in low-wage, predominantly female jobs (as well as providing higher pay in given jobs through equal pay provisions and permitting qualified women to leave low-wage jobs for high-wage jobs) if pay in such low-wage jobs responds to the changes in demand and, in particular, supply that will be set in motion by antidiscrimination measures. However, as many supporters of comparable worth have been quick to point out, that does not always happen; shortages in low-wage jobs, particularly in predominantly female low-wage jobs, do not always lead to higher wages for such jobs.

Many comparable worth advocates point to nursing as a particularly dramatic example of the failure of wages to respond to supply and demand. Although wages in nursing are said to be low, hospitals and other employers of nurses are said to suffer from severe shortages. Yet these shortages are alleged not to have led to wage increases for nurses; about all that has happened is a step-up in recruiting efforts, either of foreign nurses or via one-time-only inducements (a year's country club membership, a few months' paid rent, and so on) for first-time domestic recruits. Unfortunately, most comparable worth advocates have simply pointed out the seeming paradox inherent in situations of this kind without asking how and why such situations could have arisen or what can be done about them.

The paradox begins to make sense, however, once one considers the possibility that markets for some kinds of predominantly female jobs (e.g., nursing) have been cartelized—that, for example, hospitals and other large employers of nurses in major metropolitan areas have agreed not to compete with each other by offering higher wages to attract nurses. In effect, such cartelization amounts to a set of informal or formal areawide wage-fixing agreements. If this accurately describes the labor market for nurses, then it explains not only the alleged low pay of nurses, but also the alleged shortages of nurses, the failure of nurses' wages to rise, and the almost exclusive reliance on nonwage forms of competition for new recruits. With wages held at an artificially low level, it is not surprising that individual hospitals would like more nurses than they are able to attract (i.e., face shortages); that individual hospitals do not raise pay in an attempt to attract more nurses; or that competition in the nursing market takes the form of foreign recruitment, one-time-only sign-up bonuses, and so forth, rather than higher wages—just as competition in air travel centered on nonprice matters (seating, food, etc.) when airfares were regulated.

Is there any evidence (as opposed to mere conjecture) that markets for nurses and other predominantly female jobs have in fact been cartelized? The nursing labor market is literally a textbook example of a cartelized (or, in economic jargon, "monopsonized") labor market (Devine, 1969:542; Ehrenberg and Smith, 1982:65–66; Hurd, 1973; Link and Landon, 1975). According to one witness at recent congressional hearings, hospital administrators in Denver have colluded to fix wages (U.S. Congress, House, 1983:70). Similarly, another witness testified that employers of clerical workers in cities such as Boston and San Francisco have formed organizations, euphemistically known as consortia or study groups, whose true purpose is to engage in wage fixing in much the same way that producer cartels engage in collusive price fixing (see U.S. Congress, House, 1983:88, 96).

To the extent that labor markets are indeed cartelized—and I should emphasize that this is something about which, in general, there is very little hard evidence—then forcing wage increases in such markets need not have any adverse impact on employment. However, none of this has anything to do with whether the jobs in question are comparable to predominantly male jobs, be they pharmacist, tree trimmer, or parking lot attendant. Indeed, raising wages in cartelized, predominantly female jobs to a level above the one that would prevail in the absence of cartelization will reduce employment in such jobs (relative to the level that would prevail without cartelization), whether the higher wage level exceeds or is below the level prevailing in supposedly comparable predominantly male jobs.

What the possibility of labor market wage fixing—cartelization—does suggest is the advisability of a remedy that is quite different from both conventional antidiscrimination measures and comparable worth: enforcement and, if need be, amendment of the antitrust laws to ensure that employers cannot collude to depress wages. The existence and importance of cartelization merits serious study; application (or extension) of the antitrust laws to attack discriminatory wage fixing deserves serious consideration.

To sum up: both the short-run and long-run effects of comparable worth seem, at best, less than completely satisfactory, particularly when compared with available alternative means for addressing problems of discrimination. Roughly speaking, comparable worth would provide benefits for some women (and also men) in low-wage jobs at the expense of everyone else (other women in low-wage jobs, and both men and women in high-wage jobs). It would also increase prices and reduce output.

Suppose that a public official were to propose that employers be required to pay a tax for each female worker in their employ, with revenues from the tax being used for general purposes (e.g., reduction of the budget deficit). Women would obviously suffer severe costs in terms of reduced employment opportunities, and the associated benefits would be quite indirect. Such a proposal would rightly be attacked as preposterous.

Comparable worth is not terribly different, however; it amounts to requiring employers to pay a tax for each female worker in their employ and to using the resulting tax revenues to make payments to those women who manage to keep their jobs despite the impact of the tax on women's employment.[17] In this case, both the costs and benefits are obvious, but they are

---

[17] Note that the Equal Pay Act is also in effect a tax on female labor, and so in this respect is similar to comparable worth; faced with the prospect of having to pay the same wage to men and women doing the same job, a discriminatory employer is likely to employ only men (who produce the intangible known as maleness as well as output per se) in preference to women (who produce output but not maleness). Indeed, Nancy Barrett (1979:55)—an economist well known for her advocacy of effective antidiscrimination measures—has criticized the Equal Pay Act on precisely these grounds, arguing that the act was intended to help men compete with lower-paid women. While advocating comparable worth, Barrett has also warned that requiring pay increases for low-paid, predominantly female jobs pursuant to comparable worth will impose losses on firms and that "we can't expect firms to swallow those losses; that's crazy" (1984:32). The essential difference between the Equal Pay Act and Title VII is that the latter requires not only equal pay for equal work but also equal treatment of comparably qualified men and women with respect to hiring, assignment, promotion, and the like. Thus, under Title VII, a firm cannot avoid paying women the same wage as men are paid in a given job by simply not employing any women in that job—as would be possible under the Equal Pay Act. The essential difference between comparable worth and Title VII is that comparable worth merely makes it more expensive for firms to employ low-wage, predominantly female labor, whereas Title VII makes it more expensive for firms to engage in unequal treatment of any kind (with respect to pay, hiring, promotion, and so forth) of equally qualified men and women.

sustained or received by separate groups of women. No attempt would be made to compensate the losers from the gains of the winners; indeed, it is far from obvious that the aggregate gains of the winners would be sufficient to provide full compensation for the losers, even if such compensation were feasible. All in all, therefore, comparable worth is unlikely to appeal to large numbers of persons—but then, as has been emphasized repeatedly in this paper, there's no accounting for tastes.

ACKNOWLEDGMENT

Without implying that they necessarily share the opinions expressed herein, I thank Heidi Hartmann, Lawrence Kahn, and Cordelia Reimers for helpful comments.

REFERENCES

Abowd, J.
1984   Testimony on House Bill 1646 before the Illinois State Legislature, May 2. Graduate School of Business, University of Chicago.
Ashenfelter, O., and J. Pencavel
1976   Estimating the effects on cost and price of the elimination of sex discrimination: The case of telephone rates. Pp. 111–124 in P. Wallace, ed., *Equal Employment Opportunity and the AT&T Case*. Cambridge, Mass.: MIT Press.
Barrett, N.
1979   Women in the job market: Occupations, earnings, and career opportunities. Pp. 31–61 in R.E. Smith, ed., *The Subtle Revolution*. Washington, D.C.: Urban Institute.
1984   Poverty, welfare and comparable worth. Pp. 25–32 in P. Schlafly, ed., *Equal Pay for Unequal Work*. Washington, D.C.: Eagle Forum Education and Legal Defense Fund.
Beller, A.
1978   Title VII and the male/female earnings gap: An economic analysis. *Harvard Women's Law Journal* 1:157–173.
1980   The effect of economic conditions on the success of equal employment opportunity laws: An application to the sex differential in earnings. *Review of Economics and Statistics* 62:379–387.
1982   Occupational segregation by sex: Determinants and changes. *Journal of Human Resources* 17:371–392.
Bloom, D., and M. Killingsworth
1982   Pay discrimination research and litigation: The use of regression. *Industrial Relations* 21:318–339.
Blumrosen, R.
1979   Wage discrimination, job segregation and Title VII of the Civil Rights Act of 1964. *Journal of Law Reform* 12:399–502.
Bodner, G.
1983   Should statistics alone be allowed to prove discrimination? *Chronicle of Higher Education* June 22:56.
Brown, C.
1982   The federal attack on labor market discrimination: The mouse that roared? *Research in Labor Economics* 5:33–68.

Bureau of National Affairs
1981   *The Comparable Worth Issue*: *A BNA Special Report*. Washington, D.C.: Bureau of National Affairs.

Clauss, C.
1981   The legal issues. Pp. 80–86 and 91–94 in Equal Employment Advisory Council, *Comparable Worth*: *A Symposium on the Issues and Alternatives*. Washington, D.C.: Equal Employment Advisory Council.

Devine, E.
1969   Manpower shortages in local government employment. *American Economic Review* 59(May):538–545.

Ehrenberg, R., and R. Smith
1982   *Modern Labor Economics*. Glenview, Ill.: Scott, Foresman and Company.

Gold, M.
1983   *A Dialogue on Comparable Worth*. Ithaca, N.Y.: Industrial and Labor Relations Press.

Goldberg, M.
1982   Discrimination, nepotism, and long-run wage differentials. *Quarterly Journal of Economics* 97:307–320.

Gregory, R., and R. Duncan
1981   The relevance of segmented labor market theories: The Australian experience of the achievement of equal pay for women. *Journal of Post Keynesian Economics* 3:403–428.
1983   Equal pay for women: A reply. *Australian Economic Papers* 22:60–64.

Hartmann, H.
1984   The case for comparable worth. Pp. 11–24 in P. Schlafly, ed., *Equal Pay for Unequal Work*. Washington, D.C.: Eagle Forum Education and Legal Defense Fund.

Hurd, R.
1973   Equilibrium vacancies in a labor market dominated by non-profit firms: The "shortage" of nurses. *Review of Economics and Statistics* 55:234–240.

Johnson, G., and F. Welch
1976   The labor market implications of an economywide affirmative action program. *Industrial and Labor Relations Review* 29:508–522.

Killingsworth, M.
1984a   Testimony on comparable worth before the Joint Economic Committee, U.S. Congress, April 10. Pp. 84–127 in U.S. Congress, Joint Economic Committee, *Women in the Work Force: Pay Equity*. S. Hrg. 98-1050. Washington, D.C.: U.S. Government Printing Office.
1984b   Heterogeneous Preferences, Compensating Wage Differentials and Comparable Worth. Unpublished manuscript, Department of Economics, Rutgers University, June.
1985   Economic analysis of comparable worth and its consequences. In *Industrial Relations Research Association*, Proceedings of the Thirty-Sixth Annual Meeting. Madison, Wis.: Industrial Relations Research Association.

Killingsworth, V.
1981   What's a job worth? *Atlantic* 247 (February):10, 17.

Leonard, J.
1984a   The Impact of Affirmative Action on Employment. Working Paper No. 1310, National Bureau of Economic Research.
1984b   What Promises Are Worth: The Impact of Affirmative Action Goals. Working Paper No. 1346, National Bureau of Economic Research.

Lewin, T.
1983   The quiet allure of Alan Greenspan. *New York Times*, June 5 (Section 3):1, 12.

Link, C., and J. Landon
1975   Monopsony and union power in the market for nurses. *Southern Economic Journal* 41:498–508.
McGavin, P.
1983a   Equal pay for women: A re-assessment of the Australian experience. *Australian Economic Papers* 22:48–59.
1983b   Equal pay for women: A postscript. *Australian Economic Papers* 22:65–67.
O'Neill, J.
1983   The Determinants and Wage Effects of Occupational Segregation. Unpublished manuscript, Urban Institute, Washington, D.C.
Polachek, S.
1978   Sex differences in college major. *Industrial and Labor Relations Review* 34:498–508.
Rees, A.
1976   Compensating Wage Differentials. Pp. 336–349 in A. Skinner and T. Wilson, eds., *Essays on Adam Smith*. Oxford: Oxford University Press.
Roos, P.
1981   Sex stratification in the workplace: Male-female differences in economic returns to occupation. *Social Science Research* 10:195–224.
Schwab, D.
1980   Job evaluation and pay setting: Concepts and practices. Pp. 49–78 in R. Livernash, ed., *Comparable Worth: Issues and Alternatives*. Washington, D.C.: Equal Employment Advisory Council.
Smith, A.
1776   *The Wealth of Nations*. Reprinted 1937. E. Cannan, ed. New York: Modern Library.
Snape, R.
1980   Wage Policy and the Australian Economy in the 1970's and Beyond. Seminar Paper No. 6, Department of Economics, Flinders University of South Australia.
Treiman, D., and H. Hartmann, eds.
1981   *Women, Work, and Wages: Equal Pay for Jobs of Equal Value*. Committee on Occupational Classification and Analysis. Washington, D.C.: National Academy Press.
U.S. Congress, House
1983   *Pay Equity: Equal Pay for Work of Comparable Value*. Parts I and II, Serial No. 97–53. Committee on Post Office and Civil Service, Subcommittees on Human Resources, Civil Service and Compensation and Employee Benefits. Washington, D.C.: U.S. Government Printing Office.
Yale Law Journal
1981   Equal pay, comparable work, and job evaluation. *Yale Law Journal* 90:657–680.

Jobs, Job Status, and Women's Gains From Affirmative Action: Implications for Comparable Worth

James E. Rosenbaum

Despite affirmative action and other equal employment opportunity (EEO) efforts of the 1970s, the male-female wage gap persists. The limitations of past efforts have made us realize that the problem may be structural in origin and may be due to sex segregation in jobs and to the way jobs are compensated. Unfortunately, most social science research on pay equity has studied individuals' earnings, which may not reveal institutional mechanisms that contribute to much of the pay difference among jobs in a firm. Moreover, in a labor market in which men and women often hold entirely different jobs, the relative pay of individuals within the same jobs may be a less important source of discrimination than how different jobs are compensated across pay levels (Treiman and Hartmann, 1981). In particular, the issue of comparable worth poses the question of whether jobs held predominantly by women are undervalued, and thus undercompensated, relative to jobs of comparable worth that are held predominantly by men. Consequently, the study of pay equity must consider how the level of compensation for jobs is determined.

Compensation systems in organizations often operate by a two-stage process in which the relative value of jobs is first determined and then the relative pay of individuals within jobs is determined. The latter process involves the assessment of an individual's contribution compared with the contributions of others in the same job, and this assessment—usually by the supervisor of all these people—tends to operate in the way neoclassical economists customarily assume.

However, the former process, determining the value of jobs, requires evaluating highly different tasks and classifying them into a limited number of ranked pay levels. Since these pay levels generally confer differential social status, they may be termed *status categories* or *statuses*. This process of evaluating the worth of jobs has recently become a focus of interest but has not yet received much empirical attention. The study reported in this paper provides one of the first opportunities to examine this issue empirically.

The process of assigning differential status rankings to jobs initially evolved through traditional customs and beliefs. Some jobs were considered to have more status because they required more skill or were difficult (or for a diversity of other reasons), and this consensus on status was the basis for compensation differences. In recent decades these traditional status rankings have come under increasing criticism, and, in response, formal job evaluation systems have been devised to make the process of assigning jobs to differential hierarchical positions more objective, rational, and equitable. This change has raised the question of whether this shift from tradition to job evaluation has led to greater pay equity between jobs held predominantly by men and those held predominantly by women.

This paper describes the results of a study of these issues in a large corporation. First, the study investigates how jobs are compensated, how jobs are allocated to different status categories, and the extent to which job status prevents a narrowing of the wage gap between men and women. Second, since the corporation implemented an increasingly strong affirmative action program over the period studied, the study investigates what affirmative action has accomplished in this corporation and where it falls short. Third, since job evaluation was implemented in this firm, this study provides an opportunity to observe and draw lessons concerning the use and limitations of that tool in achieving pay equity.

Three findings are of particular importance. First, even a very strong affirmative action program that leads to very great benefits for some women may neglect other groups of women, and, in particular, it may aid the class of women but not lead to reparation for the individuals most hurt by past discrimination. Second, affirmative action may help individuals while maintaining forms of structural discrimination against female jobs that may subsequently undermine the long-term impact of affirmative action efforts. Third, reform efforts to implement job evaluation, even in the context of a strong affirmative action program, may not overcome the salary disadvantages of female jobs and, most perniciously, may inadvertently serve to legitimate traditional values under the mask of scientific procedure. These findings suggest that developing a comparable worth strategy may be necessary to improve women's earnings and that such a strategy, which requires changing job structures, is likely to be difficult to implement.

This paper is based on the results of a larger study, which is reported in a recently completed book, *Career Mobility in a Corporate Hierarchy* (Rosenbaum, 1984). In this brief paper statistical results are not discussed in detail. Readers wishing more detail about the analyses and theoretical conceptions alluded to here are referred to that book.

SETTING AND DATA

This paper is based on a study of employees' earnings and job attributes in a large corporation over a 13-year period from 1962 to 1975. The corporation employed between 10,000 and 15,000 employees in the period studied, making it slightly larger than the median corporation in *Fortune*'s 500 largest corporations. The corporation is a large, autonomous, investor-owned firm, having offices in many cities and towns across a large geographic region.

The study had use of the computerized personnel records of the corporation for the years 1962, 1965, 1969, 1972, and 1975, permitting analyses of changes over 3-year intervals for all but one period. The analyses reported here used two kinds of samples.

One set of analyses is based on independently drawn 25 percent random samples of all individuals in the firm in four periods (the 1962 data were excluded because they lacked information on race). Regression analyses were used to explain individuals' earnings (in logs, adjusted to 1967 dollars), in terms of individual attributes (experience, education, entry age, sex, race, and the status ranking of colleges attended [using the Astin 1965 scale]) and comparing their relative influences within and across job status levels.

The other set of analyses examined the determinants of the average pay that jobs offer. These analyses are based on a data set that aggregates information about all individuals in each job (i.e., a 100 percent sample) to describe jobs in terms of averages: average tenure, average earnings, percentage of college graduates, percentage female, and so forth. These analyses took jobs as the units of analysis in order to discover relationships among the attributes of jobs. The same four time periods are analyzed.

The data for these analyses were taken from the computerized file of the complete personnel records of the corporation. The availability of actual personnel records makes this research distinct from most economic and sociological research in this area and offers two important advantages. First, these personnel records offer valid and precise information on employees' salaries, levels of attainment in the organizational hierarchy, education, college attended, age, and years of experience in the corporation (tenure). Most research in this area has been based on employees' self-reports, and the possibilities of distortions or poor recollection are generally a cause of concern. In contrast, these personnel records are systematically kept by the corporation's personnel department for the organization's own use; consequently, extensive data-checking procedures have been implemented to ensure the accuracy of the information, since mistakes would have important implications for company personnel practices.

Second, these personnel records represent the complete universe of employees in the corporation. Most studies of organizations have had to rely on employees' cooperation, and less-than-perfect cooperation leads to incomplete information or possibly biased samples. For instance, Grusky's (1966) 75 percent response rate (in the data used in Halaby, 1979) is rather good as questionnaire response rates go; however, it does raise questions about the representativeness of the sample that cannot be completely settled. The data in Rosenbaum (1984) were drawn from the universe of all employees in the cohorts studied, and no information is missing (except the above-noted race information in 1962).

Of course, the use of personnel records does have its own limitations, primarily in that they do not include all the information that a researcher might like to consider. In particular, the records do not include information on marital status or actual years of education, which previous research has suggested to be worthy of consideration.

EFFECTS OF AFFIRMATIVE ACTION ON INDIVIDUALS

This organization implemented a serious affirmative action program in 1970 and an even stronger one in 1973, and these two programs had an impressive beneficial impact on women's earnings. In 1969, before these programs began, women received about 46 percent lower earnings than men with similar characteristics at entry, and their disadvantage remained at about the same magnitude for those with greater seniority. The first and second affirmative action programs increasingly reduced the female disadvantage: from 46 percent in 1969 to 39 percent in 1972 and 23 percent in 1975. Female college graduates gained even more, going from a 36 percent disadvantage for new entrants before affirmative action to only a 3 percent disadvantage by 1975.

However, more-senior women did not fully share in these gains. While seniority benefited women at the same rate as men in 1969, by 1972 their rate of earnings increase with seniority was 21 percent lower than that of men, and by 1975 it was 29 percent less. For example, in terms of the magnitude of their earnings, entering women in 1975 had a 23 percent earnings disadvantage relative to male peers, but women with just 10 years of seniority had a 31 percent disadvantage relative to male peers. At 20 years' tenure the disadvantage was even greater. Obviously the great gains for newly entering women were not being fully shared with their more senior peers.

This outcome is particularly poignant, because it was the more-senior women who had been most hurt by the previous decades of discrimination and whose experience had promoted the affirmative action program. Nonetheless, the affirmative action program was not providing reparation for the deprivation these women had experienced. The specific individuals who had been most hurt by previous discrimination were left with earnings similar to what they had always been.

As observers of the civil rights movement have noted, reforms have differential impact on various members of a deprived group. What is the reason for this discrepancy? Although individual attributes may be involved, analyses also indicate a social structural mechanism that mediated most of this discrepancy. Most of the increasing discrepancy for more-senior females was mediated by job status in the organizational hierarchy. Specifically, when job status was introduced into the earnings regression, it accounted for most of the negative effect of tenure for women (see Rosenbaum, 1984:Ch.7). Further analyses indicate that newly entering women received great increases in job status from the affirmative action program, but more-senior women continued in the same jobs or in jobs of similar low status. The job status system created an important obstacle to earnings gains for senior women.

Having found that job status played a role in preventing senior women from sharing in the benefits of affirmative action, the following analyses seek to study how jobs and the composition of jobs may contribute to this process.

THE CREATION AND DISSOLUTION OF JOBS

For the purposes of these analyses, we must define the sample of jobs to be analyzed and consider to what extent jobs are stable entities in this corporation over time. Of course, this issue has very practical implications. If the same set of jobs stably exists over time, then a one-time comparable worth reassessment will have enduring effects, while if jobs are continually being created and disbanded, then comparable worth efforts must be made on a continuing basis. Large organizations are usually conceptualized as unchanging, almost physical structures—much like the concrete and steel structures that house them. Organizational charts of jobs in an organization are portrayed as if these diagrams represented something enduring about the organization.

Yet organizations often change their organizational structures; jobs are created and destroyed. Technological and economic changes occur, requiring new kinds of jobs and making others obsolete. Political battles over authority and task responsibilities change jobs into entirely different jobs.

Individual job occupants become proficient and take on so many additional tasks that they change the nature of a particular job. These dynamic processes seem entirely plausible, but we have no idea how often they occur. To the extent that they occur, they pose a serious challenge to our notion of a fixed organizational structure, for they suggest that old job duties or old ways of organizing duties into jobs disappear and new duties or new ways of organizing duties appear in the form of new jobs. If jobs and job statuses are as important as they appear to be in affecting earnings, this degree of change in the job structure will have important implications for any program designed to affect earnings and employment outcomes.

The study analyzed the set of job titles listed in the personnel records for the years 1962, 1965, 1969, 1972, and 1975. Titles for the three lowest levels in the organization—nonmanagement, foreman, and lower management—are considered in this paper. The job title identifications for higher levels were removed from the data to protect the anonymity of employees, since these jobs tended to have few occupants. Their small size also made them unsuitable for analysis.

The main concern of the first analysis was the number of jobs that appeared or disappeared, i.e., that went from having no occupants to having some occupants, and vice versa. However, since jobs with few occupants could mistakenly appear to have been eliminated when they temporarily have several vacancies, inferences are more ambiguous with these jobs. Consequently, the analysis distinguished between small jobs (having one to four occupants) and large jobs (having five or more). We can be more confident in inferring that jobs have been eliminated when jobs with five or more occupants subsequently have no occupants.

The pattern of changes in job occupancy is one of high levels of job disappearance and creation. For example, in nonmanagement, 26 of the 95 small jobs (with one to four occupants) in 1962 had become empty 7 years later, and 4 of 76 large jobs (with five or more occupants) in 1962 had become empty 7 years later. Even more new jobs were created over these time intervals. Between 1962 and 1969, 26 small and 14 large nonmanagement jobs were created.

The patterns for other jobs show even greater amounts of job disappearance and job creation. While 67 percent of the nonmanagement jobs existing in either 1962 or 1969 were existing in both years, only 54 percent of the foreman jobs and 41 percent of the lower-management jobs were similarly enduring. For the 13-year interval between 1962 and 1975, the comparable figures were much lower for all jobs and the difference among jobs was even greater: 53 percent for nonmanagement, 46 percent for foreman, and 22 percent for lower-management jobs. For all three kinds of jobs, most jobs existing in these years were abolished or newly created over the period; persistence is more the exception than the rule.

In considering the possible generalizability of these findings, what is most striking is that this company has not undergone enormous outwardly visible changes. It continued to conduct the same activities over the entire period. Nor have there been any mergers with other companies nor divestitures of subsidiaries. To all outward appearances, it is the same organization housed in most of the same buildings doing largely the same activities over the entire decade. Nor has it had any new leadership or organizational shake-ups that would explain these changes. As large corporations go, it is probably more stable and less changed than most over the period considered.

Of course, affirmative action, job evaluation, organizational contraction, and organizational growth were important changes over these periods, but they are not sufficient to explain the changes observed. The 1962–1969 period in particular is largely unexplained by these changes, since most of them occurred after this period. Organizational growth is the main feature of the period, and, although growth may explain job creation, it does not explain why more jobs were disbanded than were created over the period. The disappearance and creation of jobs found here are indicative of small changes that gradually evolved from a multitude of particular decisions in various parts of the organization. Although no other evidence is available on this specific point, it is reminiscent of Granovetter's finding that 35 percent of the job placements in his study were jobs that had not existed previously (Granovetter, 1974:14).

These results have important implications for job evaluation programs. Although a jobs-based policy may be necessary for realizing goals for affirmative action and is essential in developing a comparable worth strategy, a lasting solution will not result from a one-time effort. With jobs continually being disbanded and created, any reform effort requires the formulation of an entirely new system and a continuing commitment to its implementation. This analysis also clearly indicates that our customary image of a fixed organizational hierarchy is seriously misleading. Jobs appear and disappear at a surprisingly high rate. White's (1970) procedure for analyzing mobility in terms of vacancy chains would clearly not apply here, even over the short period 1962 to 1969. Although the assumptions of vacancy analysis seemed to apply rather well to the hierarchy of the Episcopal church that White studied, in the corporation studied here any vacancy that occurred could go unfilled forever, while new jobs were being created and filled that had never before been occupied.

DO JOBS OFFER STABLE COMPENSATION?

To what extent do jobs change in the relative compensation they offer over periods of changing economic circumstances? The importance of jobs and job statuses to earnings will be especially great if it is found that jobs provide stable relative earnings over time.

We commonly assume that jobs retain the same value over time, so that compensation would not be very responsive to changes in economic circumstances. However, these hypotheses are put to a severe test in studying the periods included in these data, for they were times of economic and social change. The successive periods in these data were times of modest growth (1962 to 1965) followed by booming growth (1965 to 1969). We would expect such changes to be accompanied by changes in priorities among types of jobs. Furthermore, the organization shifted from a traditional job status system to a job evaluation system during this period (in 1972). In addition, an affirmative action program begun in 1970 was made even stronger in 1973—developments that we would expect to change the relative standing of jobs filled with large proportions of women and minorities. In the face of these great changes, to what extent did jobs change in the compensation they offered?

The job titles data file was created from the complete personnel records on all employees in the firm. These data on individuals were aggregated by job titles, so that jobs became the units of analysis, and the variables for these units were the average salary of all occupants in each job, the average tenure of job occupants, the percentage of job occupants with a college degree, the percentage of job occupants who were female, and so forth.

This section reports the analysis of the compensation offered by a job. This is indicated by the average earnings of all individuals who occupy the job at a particular time and is called job salary or simply salary. There is a large range of job salaries in this organization, even within a single level of the organizational hierarchy.[1] To what extent are these job salaries stable properties of jobs over these periods of great economic changes?

The analysis finds only minimal change in salaries. Job salaries in non-management levels remained extremely stable between 1962 and 1975 (Table 1). All correlations are large: the correlations of 1962 job salaries with those in later years show negligible decline (.98, .97, .96, .96). The comparable correlations at the foreman level start at the same magnitude, but the correlations of 1962 job salaries with those in later years show some decline, particularly between 1969 and 1972 (.96, .94, .88, .84). (In this and

---

[1] In the year 1962, the job salaries of nonmanagement jobs ranged from $3,354 to $8,684, with a mean of $5,462 and a standard deviation of $1,336 for the 171 jobs on that level. Foreman jobs offered job salaries in the range of $4,810 to $10,061, with a mean of $8,031 and a standard deviation of $1,511 for the 155 jobs. Lower-management job salaries were between $9,222 and $12,203 with a mean of $11,422 and a standard deviation of $729 for the 86 jobs.

TABLE 1   Stability of Job Salaries by Level (Pearson correlations)

	Nonmanagement Level			
	1962	1965	1969	1972
1965	.977			
1969	.968	.980		
1972	.958	.966	.968	
1975	.958	.954	.948	.954

	Foreman Level			
	1962	1965	1969	1972
1965	.965			
1969	.944	.952		
1972	.876	.881	.920	
1975	.842	.868	.869	.898

subsequent analyses, the lower-management level was not analyzed, because too few jobs persist over these periods.)

Despite considerable changes in economic circumstances and organizational practices over these periods, job salaries remained extremely stable for nonmanagement and foreman levels. This stability is particularly striking, for it occurred despite an explicit effort to reform the traditional job status system by implementing job evaluation at foreman levels and above. This effort was implemented in 1972 and was probably responsible for the declining earnings correlation between 1969 and 1972 at the foreman level. However, the decline in the earnings correlation is surprisingly minor, given the extensiveness of the reform. This stability suggests that the job evaluation effort had little effect on the average earnings in jobs.

THE SEX COMPOSITION OF JOBS AND WOMEN'S EARNINGS

Having seen that jobs offered highly stable salaries over this period, our analysis of the effects on women's earnings must turn to an analysis of the composition of jobs to understand how women are allocated among jobs and how this affects their earnings. We begin by describing the sex composition of jobs and how it was affected by affirmative action.

The affirmative action program had an increasingly strong effect in integrating jobs. Of the 100 nonmanagement jobs with five or more individuals in 1965, only 6 contained both men and women (Table 2). Almost 40 were all-female jobs and 55 were all-male jobs. The numbers remained similar in

TABLE 2   Jobs at Each Level by Percentage Female, 1962–1975
(for jobs with five or more employees)

Level	1962	1965	1969	1972	1975
Nonmanagement					
0 percent	47	55	42	34	19
1–99 percent	3	6	7	13	25
100 percent	23	37	34	31	31
Total	73	98	83	78	75
Foreman					
0 percent	18	25	20	17	17
1–99 percent	2	7	7	13	14
100 percent	24	27	25	18	20
Total	44	59	52	48	51
Lower-management					
0 percent	13	21	18	9	8
1–99 percent	0	0	5	4	8
100 percent	0	0	0	1	1
Total	13	21	23	14	17

the following period, but by 1972 the modest affirmative action program had doubled the number of sex-integrated jobs (to 13), and the number doubled again by 1975 (to 25). Similar changes occurred in the foreman and lower-management levels. The affirmative action program seems to have had great success in increasing the number of integrated jobs.

However, despite these gains, most jobs were unaffected. By 1975, even with a generous definition of integration as the broadest possible range (1 to 99 percent women), only one-third of nonmanagement jobs fit into this range, and only 27 percent of foreman jobs did so. Clearly, the vast majority of jobs were still segregated by sex.

Moreover, the sex-segregated jobs offered considerably different salaries. All-female jobs paid an average salary that was about three-quarters of the salary paid by all-male jobs, and this ratio applies both to nonmanagement and foreman levels in most years (Table 3). There is a general trend toward slightly greater equality over these years, but the trend is modest (and it shows an unexplainable reversal at the nonmanagement level in 1975). Female jobs clearly showed much less gain than individual women experienced over this period.

Of course, the simple association between female composition and average salary may be highly misleading, since jobs may differ in other respects

TABLE 3   Average Salary for Jobs by Percentage Female in Jobs, 1962–1975 (for jobs with five or more employees)

Level	1962	1965	1969	1972	1975
Nonmanagement					
0 percent	$ 6,268	$ 6,988	$ 7,894	$10,009	$14,679
100 percent	4,530	4,854	5,850	7,590	10,632
Foreman					
0 percent	8,863	10,050	12,345	15,297	19,713
100 percent	6,849	7,440	9,104	11,569	15,722
Lower-management					
0 percent	11,160	12,440	14,617	19,368	22,600
100 percent	—	—	—	18,333	21,985

and the apparent effects of female composition may actually be due to other factors. For instance, jobs may differ in terms of the education and training they require, and economists might suggest that the human capital composition of jobs may account for the apparent effects of female composition. Regressions were run to study the effects of female and minority composition on job salaries, controlling for the percentage of college graduates in the job and the average tenure in the job (Table 4). As economists would predict, education and training affected job salaries, but percentage minority and percentage female also had significant independent effects.

Percentage female had a strong significant negative relationship with job salaries in all years, even after controlling for human capital composition. At the nonmanagement level in 1965, jobs were paid $21 less for each additional female percentage unit, so that the regression estimates that jobs with 100 percent females were paid $2,100 less than all-male jobs, a figure very close to the real difference between the job salaries of all-male and all-female jobs. Although this difference declined over the periods of increasingly strong affirmative action, even in 1975 it retained a strong significant negative effect. At the foreman level the decline was less, and it was more erratic (perhaps because of the large influx of women promoted into foreman-level female jobs in 1972). But even in 1975 female composition still had a strong negative association with job salaries. Although human capital composition accounts for some of the earnings differences among jobs (particularly at the foreman level), even after controlling for this, jobs with a higher percentage female offered lower salaries.[2]

---

[2] The large unexplained changes in the influence of minority percentage may be due to the small numbers of minorities in most jobs.

TABLE 4   Human Capital, Sex, and Race Effects on Job Salaries Over Four Periods

Level	1965	1969	1972	1975
Nonmanagement				
Percentage college	27.814*	22.313*	25.821*	26.522*
graduates	(5.175)	(5.173)	(6.012)	(6.842)
Tenure	−.319*	−.387*	.898*	.586*
	(.099)	(.097)	(.227)	(.259)
Percentage minority	−38.045*	−22.667*	−14.207	−24.159*
	(14.112)	(7.453)	(7.898)	(8.749)
Percentage female	−20.759*	−19.868*	−14.946*	−12.310*
	(4.383)	(5.192)	(5.170)	(5.031)
Constant	75.423*	81.330*	66.212*	75.710*
	(2.874)	(3.290)	(3.640)	(4.473)
Variance explained (R^2)	43.1%	39.3%	40.3%	37.3%
Standardized coefficients				
Percentage college				
graduates	.416	.401	.390	.370
Tenure	−.248	−.376	.382	.231
Percentage minority	−.209	−.276	−.172	−.278
Percentage female	−.369	−.339	−.258	−.231
Foreman				
Percentage college	7.116*	10.718*	12.783*	11.022*
graduates	(1.906)	(3.550)	(3.907)	(3.495)
Tenure	.256*	.046	.512*	.460*
	(.103)	(.120)	(.192)	(.195)
Percentage minority	−2.623	−84.099*	−9.941	−1.147
	(13.479)	(22.241)	(6.320)	(5.737)
Percentage female	−10.259*	−8.108*	−10.200*	−8.192*
	(1.122)	(1.011)	(1.417)	(1.460)
Constant	95.278*	103.558*	103.885*	104.559*
	(2.519)	(2.966)	(4.538)	(4.841)
Variance explained (R^2)	40.0%	46.7%	41.5%	32.4%
Standardized coefficients				
Percentage college				
graduates	.224	.203	.262	.283
Tenure	.150	.025	.219	.212
Percentage minority	−.011	−.246	−.121	−.017
Percentage female	−.560	−.534	−.541	−.472

* Coefficient significant at .05 level.

TABLE 5 Human Capital, Sex, Race, and Status Effects on Job Salaries Over Four Periods

Foreman Level	1965	1969	1972	1975
Percentage college	−2.559*	−2.781	.509	−1.689
graduates	(.571)	(1.529)	(2.236)	(1.381)
Tenure	.111*	−.079	.437*	.175*
	(.029)	(.049)	(.103)	(.073)
Percentage minority	−7.646*	−26.520*	−2.172	.053
	(3.749)	(9.269)	(3.435)	(2.115)
Percentage female	−.778*	−1.681	−2.870*	−.250
	(.376)	(.480)	(.887)	(.621)
Job status	3.169*	2.989*	9.164*	9.502*
	(.070)	(.117)	(.567)	(.373)
Constant	61.949*	72.561*	69.731*	73.949*
	(1.017)	(1.704)	(3.230)	(2.151)
Variance explained (R^2)	95.4%	91.4%	83.2%	90.9%
Standardized coefficients				
Percentage college				
graduates	−.081	−.053	.010	−.043
Tenure	.065	.043	.186	.081
Percentage minority	−.035	−.078	−.026	.001
Percentage female	−.042	.111	−.152	−.014
Job status	.973	.894	.812	.949
n =	44	59	53	52

Partitioning of variance from Table 5

	Variance (%)							
	Unique	Total	Unique	Total	Unique	Total	Unique	Total
Demographic variables	1.5	40.0	2.1	46.7	5.2	41.5	1.2	32.4
Status	55.4	93.9	44.7	89.3	41.7	78.0	58.5	89.7
Shared	38.5		44.6		36.3		31.2	
Total	95.4		91.4		83.2		90.9	

* Coefficient significant at .05 level.

Moreover, further analysis indicates that the job status system was involved in mediating much of the effect of female percentage. Adding job status to this regression reduces the net effect of percentage female a great deal (Table 5). For instance, while each additional unit of female percentage reduces job salaries at the nonmanagement level by $19.87 in 1969, each female percentage unit subtracts only $1.68 after controlling for job status. This indicates that nearly all of the effect of female percentage on job salaries is due to the lower statuses of these jobs. What is most noteworthy is that this remains true even after the organization shifted from a status system based on tradition to a system based on job evaluation. In 1972, after job evaluation was implemented, each female percentage unit subtracts almost $15, but after controlling for job status, each female percentage unit subtracts less than $3. Job evaluation created a status hierarchy that continues to mediate much of the effect of female composition on earnings in the same way that the traditional status system did. Job evaluation, even in the context of a strong affirmative action program, maintains and possibly reinforces much of the earnings differences among male and female jobs.

PROMOTION CHANCES ASSOCIATED WITH JOBS

This analysis turns to another issue that is sometimes ignored in the discussion of job rewards. Jobs differ in the promotion opportunities they offer. Human capital economists might attribute this to the differential training offered by jobs, while structural sociologists would explain it in terms of opportunity structures. Regardless of cause, however, these data show that the percentage of individuals who are promoted from a given job tends to be highly stable. The percentage of employees promoted from 1962 jobs in the next 3 years is highly correlated with the percentage promoted from the same jobs a decade later ($r = .807$ at the foreman level, $.735$ at the nonmanagement level).

Moreover, jobs have lasting effects on individuals' careers. The 1975 attainments of the cohort of employees who entered this organization between 1960 and 1962 were analyzed (Rosenbaum, 1984:Ch. 6). Using separate (dummy) variables for each job, the longitudinal analysis indicates that individuals' 1962 jobs had a very large effect on their attainments 13 years later, even after controlling for sex, race, age, education, and a rough proxy measure of ability (the Astin 1965 scale of college quality). As an indication of unmeasured components of human capital, 1962 earnings were also introduced into the regression. In all analyses, early jobs continued to have a strong and significant effect on attainment 13 years later (see Rosenbaum, 1984:Ch. 6).

Moreover, this effect does more than simply advance an individual to a higher job in the following period. Even controlling for intervening attainments (in 1965), early jobs had a significant enduring effect on individuals' subsequent careers. Even employees who did not advance in their first few years still benefited from early placements in higher jobs. According to the Horatio Alger stories that are often cited in this organization, individuals who overcome initial low origins are offered advancements to the highest echelons. Analyses found that some of these individuals (who entered the firm in the years 1960 to 1962) did indeed overcome low origins by 1965 to attain the same jobs as "elites" who had been in these higher-status jobs from the outset. When their attainments 10 years later (1975) were compared, however, the Horatio Alger types ended up much lower than the elites who had been initially favored with better jobs. Early jobs have an enduring effect that even subsequent attainments do not eradicate.

Moreover, most of the effect of individual jobs was due to the way jobs are ranked in the job status system. When these analyses were repeated replacing the job dummy variables by the single job status variable, the results remained quite similar. Early job status explained nearly as much variation in later job status (or later earnings) as did dummy variables for all the individual jobs. Clearly, the job status system in this company has an important impact on employees' careers.

Given the great importance of jobs and job statuses in determining employees' careers, it is noteworthy that the promotions associated with jobs are often ignored as job effects. The reason is clear; it is not easy to determine the effects of jobs on future promotions in short-run analyses. It is clear, however, that the ultimate impact of jobs will be related to these kinds of outcomes.

The data on this firm permit an analysis of these issues. Taking as the dependent variable the percentage of employees promoted from a job in the next 3 (or 4) years, regression analyses were run using the same model as was used to explain job salaries. Controlling for percentage of college graduates and average tenure, the regressions found that the female concentration of a job was negatively related to the promotion chances of a job during the 1960s (Table 6). However, the affirmative action program had a strong effect on this result. Over the two periods in the 1970s, the negative influence of percentage female continually decreased at the nonmanagement level, and at the foreman level its influence vanished in the 1969–1972 period and actually became significantly positive in the final period. Moreover, when job status was added to this regression, the effect of percentage female on 1969–1972 promotions declined slightly and had no effect at all on 1972–1975 promotions (Table 7). In spite of the high stability of promotion rates offered by jobs, the stability is not total, and jobs with high proportions of women experienced a large reduction in their disadvantage.

These results may be interpreted as reassuring in some respects. While

TABLE 6   Human Capital, Sex, and Race Effects on the Promotion Chances of Jobs Over Four Periods

Level	1962-1965	1965-1969	1969-1972	1972-1975
Nonmanagement				
Percentage college	.688*	1.167*	.584*	.697*
graduates	(.095)	(.223)	(.171)	(.091)
Tenure	.005	−.002	−.004	−.001
	(.005)	(.004)	(.003)	(.003)
Percentage minority	—	.823	.172	−.096
		(.606)	(.247)	(.122)
Percentage female	−.108	−.321	−.140	−.114
	(.169)	(.218)	(.184)	(.084)
Constant	.141	.380*	.351*	.114*
	(.078)	(.123)	(.109)	(.056)
Variance explained (R^2)	42.7%	24.7%	12.9%	45.3%
Standardized coefficients				
Percentage college				
graduates	.655	.466	.382	.665
Tenure	.083	−.050	−.132	−.036
Percentage minority	—	.121	.075	−.073
Percentage female	−.057	−.131	−.081	−.117
n =	76	101	85	81
Foreman				
Percentage college	.439*	.491*	.369*	.473*
graduates	(.105)	(.079)	(.104)	(.034)
Tenure	.001	.001	.000	−.004
	(.003)	(.004)	(.003)	(.003)
Percentage minority	—	−1.368	−.419	−.432*
		(1.401)	(.314)	(.185)
Percentage female	−.085	−.136	.010	.069*
	(.071)	(.082)	(.065)	(.032)
Constant	.029	.129	.065	.084
	(.086)	(.096)	(.067)	(.056)
Variance explained (R^2)	39.0%	50.6%	35.6%	86.1%
Standardized coefficients				
Percentage college				
graduates	.591	.650	.556	.888
Tenure	.023	.015	.010	−.095
Percentage minority	—	−.095	−.158	−.143
Percentage female	−.154	−.165	.019	.120
n =	43	59	53	50

* Coefficient significant at .05 level.

percentage female and job status remained serious obstacles to earnings parity, they did not limit women's promotions after the affirmative action program began. Jobs with high proportions of women had as high or higher promotion rates as jobs with high proportions of men.

However, although these specific results are gratifying, some caution is required. The high rates of female promotions that were demanded by the organization's affirmative action program are unlikely to be maintained after the organization reaches its initial targets and the impetus for the affirmative action program subsides. At that time it may be expected that the organization will go back to more selectivity in its promotions of women, and then the customary reliance on job status for promotions will once again hurt individuals in the low-ranked, predominantly female jobs. Although the promotion findings are reassuring in the short run, even these findings call for some concern about how the job evaluation system is ranking female jobs. Our awareness of the traditional historical relationship between job status and promotions suggests that one must be wary about whether the new pattern will endure.

CONCLUSIONS

This study sought to discover how jobs and job statuses affect women's earnings and how they affect women's gains from an affirmative action program. At the individual level the analyses indicate that job status is an important determinant of women's earnings. The job status system determined which women benefit and which do not benefit from the strong affirmative action program. In particular, the job status system prevented more-senior women from gaining as much from the affirmative action program as their less-senior peers.

In order to get another perspective on job effects, the properties of jobs were investigated. The continual appearance of new jobs clearly suggests that lasting reforms will not result from one-time efforts. Reforms must be embodied in coherent systems, like job evaluation systems, that can continue to handle the many new jobs that are created.

The findings also indicate the need for revaluing the worth of jobs. In the 1960s the female composition of jobs had a strong negative influence on job salaries. While previous research has shown such a relationship for occupational groups (Sanborn, 1964; Fuchs, 1971; Oaxaca, 1973; Sommers, 1974; Treiman and Terrell, 1975; Featherman and Hauser, 1976; Blau, 1977; Treiman et al., 1984; Roos, 1981), it has not been possible to study it for jobs within firms. The finding of female job composition effects on job salaries is particularly noteworthy because these analyses control not only for human capital composition but also for level in the authority hierarchy.

TABLE 7   Human Capital, Sex, Race, and Status Effects on the Promotion Chances of Jobs Over Four Periods

Foreman Level	1962–1965	1965–1969	1969–1972	1972–1975
Percentage college graduates	.332* (.109)	.347* (.081)	.280* (.105)	.456* (.039)
Tenure	.002 (.003)	−.001 (.004)	.000 (.003)	−.004 (.003)
Percentage minority	—	−.894 (1.271)	.049 (.352)	−.362 (.199)
Percentage female	−.005 (.074)	−.027 (.080)	.092 (.070)	.077* (.033)
Job status	.014* (.006)	.021* (.006)	.014* (.006)	.008 (.009)
Constant	−.053 (.088)	−.039 (.100)	−.095 (.090)	.054 (.064)
Variance explained (R^2)	47.1%	60.8%	43.2%	86.4%
Standardized coefficients				
Percentage college graduates	.444	.460	.422	.857
Tenure	−.077	−.032	−.009	−.100
Percentage minority	—	−.063	.019	−.120
Percentage female	−.009	.032	.166	.136
Job status	.344	.401	.391	.064
n =	43	59	53	50

* Coefficient significant at .05 level.

Moreover, the job status hierarchy mediates most of the effect of female composition on job salaries. Clearly, some revision of the job status system is necessary if women's jobs are to be better paid.

However, job evaluation does not necessarily contribute to gains for women. The findings indicate that job evaluation, even in the context of a strong affirmative action program, does not diminish the relationship between female composition and job salary very much. Indeed, the new job status system—based on job evaluation—continued to mediate this relationship.

Two kinds of cautions need to be borne in mind in evaluating these findings. First, the evidence is not sufficient to identify unambiguously whether the effect is indeed discrimination. That requires far more detailed data than this research, like most research, encompasses. However, the discrepancy between the gains of some individual women and the lack of gains for other women and for female jobs in general suggests that structural barriers may be operating, although other interpretations are possible.

Second, since this is a case study of only a single corporation, it is difficult to assess the generalizability of most of these findings. The initial finding of this study—that job status mediates most of the female earnings disadvantage—has been shown in studies of other organizations (Malkiel and Malkiel, 1973; Halaby, 1979), but its effect in preventing senior women from gaining from affirmative action and in mediating the influence of female composition requires further replication. Similarly, the effect of female composition on salaries has previously been shown for occupations but not for jobs, and it has not been possible before to relate it so clearly to job evaluation status categories.

However, regardless of generalizability, the primary value of these findings is in suggesting some issues to consider in assessing the effectiveness of affirmative action programs and in developing comparable worth strategies. Three central conclusions are stressed. First, even a very strong affirmative action program that leads to very great benefits for some women may neglect other groups of women. In particular, aiding women as a class may not lead to reparation for those most hurt by past discrimination.

Second, to the extent that these programs are based on helping individual women, as most such programs are, they are likely to have the problem observed, namely, helping some individual women while maintaining structural discrimination against female jobs. Not only does this prevent the individuals in these jobs from receiving the full benefit of the affirmative action program, but also, more seriously, it remains a structural component of the organization so that when the impetus of the affirmative action program ends, the structure may again tend to recreate old patterns.

Third, reform efforts to implement job evaluation, even in the context of a strong affirmative action program, may not overcome the salary disadvantages of female jobs. The conclusion to the interim report of the National Research Council's Committee on Occupational Classification and Analysis warned that job evaluation systems use several procedures that raise questions about whether they can be effective in fairly assessing sex-segregated jobs (Treiman, 1979:48). In particular, their reliance on market wage rates and subjective judgments raises serious risks that job evaluation will recreate the same biases as traditional status systems. Unfortunately, the present findings provide empirical support for this warning, and they suggest that job evaluations may be especially pernicious in providing legitimation for traditional values under the mask of scientific procedure.

Obviously, the ultimate answer to this problem is to integrate all sex-segregated jobs. This is a noble goal, but it is one that seems to proceed slowly. Short of that ideal, the solutions are more difficult.

Presumably, subjective job assessments and market-based factor weightings had important influences on these findings, and these may be the best targets for policy change. We currently lack sufficient evidence on how these procedures operate. However, the present findings suggest that the mechanisms underlying job evaluation need to be scrutinized to discover whether the inequalities are inequitable, and, if so, how job evaluations could be done in other ways to lead to more equitable results.

In the absence of data for analyzing the job evaluation process in detail, this study offers empirical support to the warning of the National Research Council report: jobs and job evaluation programs, even in the context of very serious and effective affirmative action programs, may partially undermine the goals of affirmative action and legitimize these inequalities. Given the difficulty of criticizing job evaluation programs, this may be a serious obstacle to preserving parity after the impetus for affirmative action programs is reduced. It also suggests caution in relying on "unreformed" job evaluation plans in comparable worth strategies. Those seeking a realignment of the wage rates of women's jobs should attempt to ensure that the job evaluation instrument used is not unfairly biased toward maintaining the status quo.

ACKNOWLEDGMENT

The author is indebted to the conference participants—particularly Bill Bielby, Heidi Hartmann, and Don Treiman—for their helpful suggestions. Preparation of this paper was supported by the Center for Urban Affairs and Policy Research at Northwestern University and by the Russell Sage Foundation. The views presented here are, of course, those of the author.

REFERENCES

Blau, Francine D.
1977   *Equal Pay in the Office.* Lexington, Mass.: Lexington Books.
Featherman, David L., and Robert M. Hauser
1976   Sexual inequalities and socioeconomic achievement in the U.S., 1962–1973. *American Sociological Review* 41 (June): 462–483.
Fuchs, Victor
1971   Differences in hourly earning between men and women. *Monthly Labor Review* 94(May):9–15.

Granovetter, Mark
   1974   *Getting a Job: A Study of Contacts and Careers.* Cambridge, Mass.: Harvard University
           Press.
Grusky, Oscar
   1966   Career mobility and organizational commitment. *Administrative Science Quarterly*
           10:489–502.
Halaby, Charles N.
   1979   Sexual inequality in the workplace: An employer-specific analysis of pay differences.
           Social Science Research 8:79–104.
Malkiel, Burton G., and Judith A. Malkiel
   1973   Male-female differentials in professional employment. *American Economic Review*
           63:693–705.
Oaxaca, Ronald
   1973   Sex discrimination in wages. Pp. 124–151 in Orley Ashenfelter and Albert Rees, eds.,
           Discrimination in Labor Markets. Princeton, N.J.: Princeton University Press.
Roos, Patricia A.
   1981   Sex stratification in the workplace: Male-female differences in economic returns to
           occupation. *Social Science Research* 10:(3).
Rosenbaum, James E.
   1984   *Career Mobility in a Corporate Hierarchy.* New York: Academic Press.
Sanborn, H.
   1964   Pay differences between men and women. *Industrial and Labor Relations Review*
           17(July):534–550.
Sommers, Dixie
   1974   Occupational rankings for men and women by earnings. *Monthly Labor Review* 97
           (August):34–51.
Treiman, Donald J.
   1979   *Job Evaluation: An Analytic Review.* Committee on Occupational Classification and
           Analysis. Washington, D.C.: National Academy of Sciences.
Treiman, Donald J., and Heidi I. Hartmann, eds.
   1981   *Women, Work, and Wages: Equal Pay for Jobs of Equal Value.* Committee on Occupa-
           tional Classification and Analysis. Washington, D.C.: National Academy Press.
Treiman, Donald J., and Kermit Terrell
   1975   Women, work, and wages—Trends in the female occupational structure since 1940. Pp.
           157–200 in Kenneth C. Land and Seymour Spilerman, eds., *Social Indicator Models.*
           New York: Russell Sage Foundation.
Treiman, Donald J., Heidi I. Hartmann, and Patricia A. Roos
   1984   Assessing pay discrimination using national data. In Helen Remick, ed., *Comparable
           Worth and Wage Discrimination: Technical Possibilities and Political Realities.* Phila-
           delphia: Temple University Press.
White, Harrison C.
   1970   *Chains of Opportunity.* Cambridge, Mass.: Harvard University Press.

Prospects for Pay Equity
in a Changing Economy

Pamela Stone Cain

INTRODUCTION

The increase in women's labor force participation, which has been especially rapid since World War II, has been characterized as a "subtle revolution" (R.E. Smith, 1979). Equally subtle and dramatic have been other trends, which, together with the increase in women's employment, have resulted in a reconfiguration of the U.S. economy and work force. One source of these trends is the fundamental transformation that has occurred as the United States moves from a manufacturing to an increasingly service-based, more technologically sophisticated economy. A second source of change is postwar demographic trends in fertility, household and family structure, and immigration. In this paper I focus on features of this ongoing transformation as they have particular relevance for the status of women and their chances for achieving parity with men in wages and jobs.

To date, women's progress in the labor market has been slow. Despite their increased labor force participation and the passage of legislation to prohibit sex discrimination in employment (the Equal Pay Act in 1963 and Title VII of the Civil Rights Act in 1964), the earnings gap between full-time, year-round male and female workers has decreased only a few percentage points in recent decades (Norwood, 1984). Moreover, although the job titles held by women have proliferated (U.S. Department of Labor, 1982), they remain concentrated in fewer jobs than men. Will future trends in the labor force and economy tend to accelerate the progress toward parity that women workers have made—facilitating job integration and closing the wage gap—or will they tend to halt or reverse it? There are no easy answers to this question. Given the scope and complexity of the factors involved, the sometimes contradictory research findings, and the difficulty of predicting the future, different interpretations and outlooks are possible. In this paper I develop alternative scenarios, beginning by reviewing recent and projected trends in women's labor force participation as well as other changes that affect the composition of the work force. Next I turn to a consideration of changes in the U.S. industrial and occupational structure as these affect the opportunities open to women. Finally, against the background of changes in labor supply and demand, I review trends in job segregation and the wage gap to assess women's progress to date and speculate about their prospects for the future. The competing interpretations that I offer highlight what is perhaps the only conclusion to be drawn: that the slow and incremental gains women workers have made cannot be taken for granted, nor can their progress be assumed to proceed as an inevitable corollary of their continued, significant presence in the labor force. I conclude by offering suggestions for needed research that would enable us to better address and illuminate these critical issues.

A NOTE ON THE PROJECTIONS USED IN THE PAPER

This paper makes use of the economic projections to 1995 compiled by the U.S. Bureau of Labor Statistics (BLS) as the basis for future scenarios (Bureau of Labor Statistics, 1984a). These projections have been criticized for failing to take into account factors in labor force growth such as the attractiveness of jobs as well as for ignoring the complementarity of men's and women's labor supply decisions (Lloyd and Niemi, 1979). Notwithstanding the validity of these criticisms, BLS projections are nonetheless useful because of their comprehensiveness and accessibility; moreover, they are periodically updated. The most recent projections replace those issued in 1980 and incorporate new information from the last census. Specifically, the 1984 revisions reflect new assumptions about longer life expectancy and higher levels of net migration as well as lower assumptions about fertility levels. These changes result in an assumption of higher overall population growth.

With regard to labor force projections, the most notable change in the 1984 estimates occurred for women ages 25 to 34. Although BLS has consistently underestimated the participation of this group, in the new projections the labor force participation rate was lowered 2 percentage points to

81.7.[1] This group still shows the largest projected increase of any labor group. Projected rates for men ages 35 to 54 and women age 35 and older were revised upward (Fullerton and Tschetter, 1984:7–8).

The basic methodology used in these forecasts is discussed fully elsewhere (Bureau of Labor Statistics, 1982b). Briefly, BLS develops three sets of projections, labeled "low," "moderate," and "high" growth. Each set entails slightly different assumptions about fiscal and monetary policy and future growth rates in the gross national product (GNP), given industries, occupations, and segments of the labor force. Labor force projections are based on population projections prepared by the Bureau of the Census. Economic projections are based on an econometric model developed by Chase Econometrics (see Andreassen et al., 1984, for details). In comparing projections generated by alternative models, BLS concluded that their estimates of future labor force growth and composition were more sensitive to demographic than to economic assumptions.

BLS cautions that "none of the three projections should be favored as the most likely" (Andreassen et al., 1984:9). Rather, the set of forecasts is intended to generate a reasonable range of possibilities. For purposes of this paper and following BLS convention, I present the estimates from the moderate growth scenario. These assume continued economic recovery from the recent recession, with real GNP increasing at an annual average of 3.2 percent through 1990, falling to 2.5 percent through the mid-1990s. For the two periods, unemployment rates of 6.3 percent and 6 percent are assumed, respectively, which seem low in light of recent experience. Given the past

---

[1] A set of projections of women's labor force participation developed by Waite (1978), which takes into account the influence of changing sex-role attitudes as well as demographic considerations, predicts an increase in labor force participation rates from 1975 to 1990 in the range of 0.7 to 5.7. From 1985 to 1990, BLS's moderate growth projection shows a change of 5.7 points. Projections by R.E. Smith (1979), which take account of women's marital status and childbearing as well as other demographic factors, are compared below with the BLS projections used in this paper:

Female Labor Force Participation Rate Projected to 1990

	Smith	BLS
Ages 16–24	67.1	69.1
Ages 25–54	68.6	75.6
Age 55 +	21.2	20.5
Total	54.8	58.3

Smith's projections also agree substantially with those of BLS, which are slightly higher, especially among women ages 25 to 54. These comparisons indicate that in its most recent set of projections, BLS may have taken steps to remedy its perennial underestimation of women's labor force participation.

record of BLS of underestimating women's economic activity and because there is error inherent in any such projection, the data presented below should be interpreted broadly, as indicative of general trends and patterns rather than as precise estimates of absolute levels and rates.

THE CHANGING DEMOGRAPHY OF THE LABOR FORCE

Four major factors shape the composition of the future labor force. First, historical shifts in fertility have resulted in a cycle of baby "boom" and "bust," with corresponding differences in the size of birth cohorts. A second factor is the different age structures and fertility of population subgroups; black and Hispanic populations are younger, exhibit higher fertility, and consequently have higher rates of growth than whites have. A third is the changing roles of women: increasing numbers are entering the paid labor force and becoming heads of households. Finally, recent upswings in the number of immigrants (both documented and undocumented) have an impact, which is difficult to measure, on the age, sex, and ethnic profile of workers.

Table 1 shows civilian labor force participation rates of different groups for 1982 and projected to 1995. Following an already-established trend toward convergence, the labor force participation rate of women is expected to increase from 52.6 percent in 1982 to about 60.3 percent in 1995. Over the same period, men's participation rate is expected to decline from 76.6 percent to 76.1 percent. The rate of convergence is most pronounced among prime-age workers ages 25 to 54. As a result of these changes, BLS forecasts that women will account for nearly two-thirds of labor force growth through the mid-1990s, i.e., two out of three first-time labor force entrants or reentrants will be women.

For both blacks and whites, increases in labor force participation will be greater among women than men, although increases for black women, whose labor force participation rates have been high historically, are not as large as those seen for whites. One out of four new or returning workers will be of black or minority background.

One implication of increased participation among women ages 24 to 54 is that more and more mothers of young children will be working. Generally there will be increasingly smaller differences in labor force activity among women by marital and family status. From 1950 to 1983, the labor force participation rates of married women with husband present and children under age 6 increased fourfold, from 11.9 to 49.9 percent. Those of women with children ages 6 to 17 more than doubled, from 28.3 to 63.8 percent (Waldman, 1984). In a special set of projections developed by BLS for women ages 20 to 34 (an age group for which differentials by marital status

TABLE 1   Civilian Labor Force Participation Rates by Sex, Age, and Race, 1982 and Projected to 1995

| Labor Group | Participation Rate | | Percentage Difference |
	1982	1995	1982–1995
Men	76.6	76.1	−0.5
16–24	72.6	74.5	+1.9
16–19	56.7	62.9	+6.2
20–24	84.9	84.1	−0.8
25–54	94.0	93.4	−0.6
25–34	94.7	93.1	−1.6
35–44	95.3	95.3	0.0
45–54	91.2	91.1	−0.1
55 and over	43.8	35.3	−8.5
55–64	70.2	64.5	−5.7
65+	17.8	13.3	−4.5
Women	52.6	60.3	+7.7
16–24	62.0	71.6	+9.6
16–19	51.4	58.2	+6.8
20–24	69.8	82.0	+12.2
25–54	66.3	78.7	+12.4
25–34	68.0	81.7	+13.7
35–44	68.0	82.8	+14.8
45–54	61.6	69.5	+7.9
55+	22.7	19.9	−2.8
55–64	41.8	42.5	+0.7
65+	7.9	7.0	−0.9
White	64.3	68.1	+3.8
Men	77.4	77.0	−0.4
16–24	74.9	79.1	+4.2
25–54	94.9	94.5	−0.4
55+	44.2	35.6	−8.6
Women	52.4	60.0	+7.6
16–24	64.7	75.4	+10.7
25–54	66.1	78.7	+12.6
55+	22.4	19.5	−2.9
Black and other	61.6	65.7	+4.1
Men	1.0	70.6	−0.4
16–24	60.0	52.7	−7.3
25–54	88.0	87.2	−0.8
55+	40.5	32.6	−7.9
Women	53.9	61.7	+7.8
16–24	48.8	55.3	+6.5
25–54	67.9	78.7	+10.8
55+	25.5	22.8	−2.7
Total, age 16+	64.0	67.8	+3.8

SOURCE: Fullerton and Tschetter (1984:Table 1).

have been greatest), married women's labor force participation is expected to increase almost 20 percentage points from 61.6 percent in 1982 to 80.3 percent in 1995. Over the same period, the rate for unmarried (including single, divorced, widowed, and separated) women will increase only 6 percentage points, to 83.2 in 1995 (Fullerton and Tschetter, 1984). Thus, in less than 20 years, marriage and childbearing are expected to exert almost no inhibiting effect on women's participation in the labor force.

Other changes in the household and family, especially the increase in single parenting, have implications for women's future labor force activity. In 1983, 59.6 percent of women with families worked, including 55.2 percent of women with children under age 6 (Johnson and Waldman, 1984). Moreover, from 1970 to 1983, the number of female heads of household in the labor force doubled. According to Johnson and Waldman, the record numbers of marriages, divorces, and subsequent labor force entry during this period are, like other changes in the labor force, a function of the activities of the baby boom cohort. By the 1980s, "divorcees—who have the highest LFP [labor force participation] rate of any marital category—had replaced widows (who have the lowest) as the largest group of women maintaining families" (Johnson and Waldman, 1984:16).

The resulting composition of the labor force is shown in Table 2. With women accounting for nearly two-thirds of labor force growth, they are expected to increase their proportion of the labor force from 43 to 46 percent. Minority representation is expected to grow slightly, to 14 percent. The proportion of white men in the labor force is projected to decline by 4 percent by 1995. By 1983 their majority had already been eclipsed: they made up only 49.8 percent of the work force (Serrin, 1984).

The age structure of the labor force is also changing. As the baby boom cohort matures, prime-age workers will make up a larger share of the work force, and the median age of labor force participants will increase: from 34.8 years old in 1982 to 37.3 in 1995 (Fullerton and Tschetter, 1984). Simultaneously, younger workers ages 16 to 24 (the baby bust cohort) will decline both in absolute numbers and proportionally. In addition, because of race and ethnic differences in fertility and age structure, blacks and other minorities will make up a greater fraction of the future youth work force.

Immigration has also contributed to changes in labor force composition. Since the 1930s, immigration has increased fivefold, and in recent years the annual legal inflow has been about 2.2 immigrants per 1,000 population (Chiswick, 1982), an average of 400,000 people per year (Keely, 1979). Not only has the pace of immigration quickened in recent years, but its nature has changed as well. Since the late 1960s, nations in Asia, Latin America, and the Caribbean have become the most important countries of origin, accounting for 61 percent of immigrants over the period 1971 to 1978

TABLE 2   Labor Force Composition: Percentage Distribution of Different Race, Sex, and Age Groups, 1982 and Projected

Labor Group	1982	1990	1995
White			
Men	50	47	46
16–24	10	8	7
25–54	32	34	34
55+	7	6	6
Women	37	39	39
16–24	9	7	7
25–54	23	27	28
55+	5	4	4
Total	(87%)	(86%)	(86%)
Black and other			
Men	7	7	7
16–24	2	1	1
25–54	4	5	5
55+	1	1	1
Women	6	7	7
16–24	1	1	1
25–34	4	5	6
55+	1	1	1
Total	(13%)	(14%)	(14%)

NOTE: Percentages may not add to 100 due to rounding.
SOURCE: Computed from Fullerton and Tschetter (1984:Table 1).

(Chiswick, 1982). Moreover, undocumented or illegal immigration has substantially increased. Estimates of illegal immigration vary widely (Keely, 1979), but the Bureau of the Census reports that there are between 3.5 million and 6 million illegal aliens in the United States, about half of them from Mexico (Chiswick, 1982). Thus, recent immigrants are young, of Hispanic or other minority background, and, by virtue of the self-selective nature of migration, have high rates of economic activity.

Key features of the labor force of the future can be summarized in light of these trends:

• Continued erosion of the prototypical white male worker's share of the labor force;
• Maturing (but not graying) of the work force as the baby boom cohort ages and enters the years of prime work life;
• A relative shortfall in the supply of younger workers or new labor force entrants;

• A reinforcement of already-established trends in female labor force participation by marital and family status, with more and more wives, mothers of young children, and heads of household entering or reentering the labor force; and

• An unknown impact of immigration, but one probably adding to the numbers of younger and minority workers.

TRENDS IN LABOR FORCE ACTIVITY
AMONG EMPLOYED WORKERS

Although there are no projections available for indicators of labor force activity among employed workers, a review of recent trends gives some idea of where things might be moving.

Hours and Weeks Worked

The BLS projections assume a continued increase in part-time employment across all employed workers through the 1990s, with a drop in average weekly hours from 35.1 in 1982 to 33.1 in 1995 (Personick, 1984). Reflecting this trend, part-time work (defined as fewer than 35 hours per week) is a small but growing phenomenon among employed men (see Table 3). Correspondingly, there has been a drop in the length of men's average work week.

Although most employed women, like men, work full time, women have been about two or three times more likely than men to work part time. Women, however, are slightly more likely than men to be working on part-time schedules involuntarily because of slack work, the inability to find a full-time job, or other reasons (U.S. Department of Labor, 1982).

TABLE 3   Part-Time Status and Average Hours of Adults at Work in Nonagricultural Industries, by Sex, 1968–1980

	Men		Women	
Year	% Part Time	Average Total Weekly Hours at Work	% Part Time	Average Total Weekly Hours at Work
1968	5.2	43.5	23.5	35.6
1970	6.3	42.6	24.5	34.9
1972	6.4	43.0	24.7	35.3
1974	6.7	42.6	25.0	35.1
1976	7.3	42.4	25.2	35.0
1978	6.9	42.8	24.7	35.3
1980	8.0	42.1	24.9	35.3

SOURCE: Computed from Bureau of Labor Statistics (1982a: Table B-22).

TABLE 4   Percentage of Part-Time Employment
Among Women, by Marital Status, March 1983

Marital Status	% Part Time
Never married	35.3
Married, husband present	29.7
Other marital status	19.5
Married, husband absent	20.1
Widowed	33.7
Divorced	13.3

SOURCE: Computed from Bureau of Labor Statistics (1984b:Table B-1).

The increase in women's labor force participation over the last 20 years has not been accompanied by a shift to more full-time work. Over the period 1968 to 1980 (see Table 3), the proportion of women on part-time schedules remained steady at about 25 percent, as did their average hours worked per week at about 35. This reflects in good measure the activities of married women.

Marital status is, in fact, a major determinant of hours worked. In 1983, 83 percent of women who were single heads of household worked full time (Johnson and Waldman, 1984). In contrast, among women with spouse present, only about 70 percent did so. Part-time work was more prevalent among never-married women (on average, these are younger workers, many of whom are also in school), widows, and married women with husband present than it was among divorced women or married women with husband absent (see Table 4).

For married women, the presence of children also increases the likelihood of part-time work. In 1980 almost 40 percent of those with children under age 18 worked part time (see Table 5). Although there was little variation in part-time employment by age of children, mothers of preschool-age children, who are presumably younger than those with older children, were only slightly more likely than mothers of school-age children to work part time, reflecting a general trend toward greater labor force attachment among younger women workers.

It should be noted that the large sex differences in part-time and full-time status do not translate into big differences in the number of hours actually worked. As Table 3 shows, in 1980 women worked an average of only about 7 fewer hours per week than men. Moreover, the foregoing discussion understates somewhat the work time of both women and men, because hours worked are reported for the primary job. In 1980 roughly 6 percent of employed men and 4 percent of employed women held two or more jobs. Among men the proportion of multiple jobholders has remained fairly stable

TABLE 5   Percentage of Part-Time Employment
Among Married Women With Work Experience,
Husband Present, 1980

Women with:	% Part Time
No children under age 18	26.9
Children under age 18	37.4
Children ages 6–17	36.8
Children under age 6	38.2
Children ages 3–5	37.6
Children under age 3	38.6
Total	32.8

SOURCE: Bureau of Labor Statistics (1983b:Table B-8).

TABLE 6   Year-Round Work Experience of Men and
Women: Percentage Working 50 to 52 Weeks Part Time
or Full Time, 1950–1981

Year	Men	Women
1950	68.5	45.0
1955	71.5	48.1
1960	68.4	46.9
1965	71.8	47.9
1970	70.5	50.7
1975	68.2	53.1
1980	69.6	56.6
1981	69.1	57.0

SOURCE: Computed from Bureau of Labor Statistics (1982a:Table C-2).

since the 1960s; among women it has nearly doubled (Bureau of Labor
Statistics, 1982a:Table C-17). Increasingly, women are seeking additional
jobs to supplement part-time work or low-paying full-time jobs (Sekscenski,
1981), and these extra hours of work are not reflected in the statistics cited
above.

In contrast to data on hours worked, data on women's year-round attachment to the labor force (weeks worked per year) reveal notable changes and a
narrowing of sex differences. While the proportion of men working year-
round has held steady since 1950 at about 70 percent (see Table 6), the
proportion of women doing so has increased substantially from 45 to 57
percent.

As with hours worked, the year-round labor force attachment of women is
affected by marital status and the presence of children. As Table 7 shows,
among full-time workers the year-round attachment of both married and
ever-married women has increased substantially since 1960. Although the

TABLE 7   Women With Year-Round Work Experience: Percentage Who
Worked Full Time, 50 to 52 Weeks, by Marital Status, 1960–1981

Marital Status	1960	1970	1980	1981
Single	38.6	33.6	37.6	37.3
Married, spouse present	33.0	40.3	44.1	45.0
Widowed, divorced, separated	46.9	51.1	55.9	56.0

SOURCE: Computed from Bureau of Labor Statistics (1982a:Table C-3).

rate of change among married women was greater than that for widowed,
separated, or divorced women, the latter group maintained significantly
higher levels of year-round activity throughout the period.

Among married women with spouse present who were full-time workers
in 1980, 53 percent of those with no children under age 18 worked 50 to 52
weeks, while for those with children the comparable figure was 37 percent.
Among women with children under age 6, only 31 percent worked year-
round (Bureau of Labor Statistics, 1983b:Table B-8). Combining part-time
and full-time workers, a similar pattern is seen: women with children,
especially preschoolers, have a tendency to work fewer weeks per year
(Bureau of Labor Statistics, 1982a:Table C-17).

Other Indicators of Labor Force Attachment

Changes in women's labor force participation rates and year-round attachment translate into the accumulation of more work experience and longer
work lives. Successively younger cohorts of women have higher participation rates. Moreover, new labor force entrants appear to be a declining
proportion of all women workers (Lloyd and Niemi, 1979). In 1950 the
average work-life expectancy of a 20-year-old woman was 14.5 years. In
1977 a 20-year-old could expect to spend 26 (almost twice as many) years
working (S.J. Smith, 1982). Men's work-life expectancy, meanwhile,
dropped from 41.5 years to 37 years. Given sex differences in life expectancy, these numbers represent an increase from 27 to 65 percent of women's
life-span versus a decrease from 85 to 72 percent of men's (Bureau of Labor
Statistics, 1983a:12). Thus, by this indicator, too, there is growing similarity between the labor force profiles of men and women.[2]

---

[2] The methods used to estimate average work life expectancy have undergone revision over the
years, so these comparisons are intended to be suggestive only. Recent work-life estimates use an
increment-decrement working life table approach that takes into account the age-specific mortality
and labor force entry and exit rates that prevailed in 1977 (S.J. Smith, 1983:36). See S.J. Smith
(1982, 1983) and Finch (1983) for a discussion of the relative strengths and weaknesses of current
methodology.

Differences between men and women still persist, however, in length of service with a particular employer—job tenure. Although sex differences in tenure are narrowing, and they no longer exist among workers up to their mid-30s, as of 1983 average tenure for employed women was 3.3 years compared with 5.1 for men (Mellor, 1984). A recent analysis of sex differences in turnover found that, while women were more likely than men to quit a job to leave the labor force, their intralabor-force mobility (leaving one job to take another) was actually lower than that of men (Haber et al., 1983). Moreover, these results corroborated others (Viscusi, 1980; Blau and Kahn, 1981) in finding that when differences in type of job, wages, part-time status, age, and family characteristics were taken into account, women did not have higher separation rates (which included permanent layoffs) than those of men. Facilitating this trend toward increased work experience is growing convergence in the unemployment rates of men and women (Bureau of Labor Statistics, 1983a), which has been attributed to women's location in what are sometimes called recession-proof industries.

Women are also increasing their education and, in terms of median years of schooling, are now on a par with men. Although they continue to surpass men in rates of high school graduation, they still lag behind them with regard to college and postgraduate training (see Table 8).

In summary, although there is increasing similarity in the labor supply of employed men and women workers, differences persist. This is especially true with regard to part-time work, where marital and family responsibilities still constrain the ability or desire of married women with children to work full time, while impelling husbands and single heads of household to do so. Women are improving their standing relative to men on various productivity-enhancing characteristics such as work experience and education, progress being greatest among younger cohorts of workers.

EVOLUTION IN THE ECONOMIC STRUCTURE

Industry Outlook

Women workers have long been concentrated in particular industries (Norwood, 1984). For most of these industries BLS projects considerable growth. Service industries are expected to create three out of every four new jobs between now and 1995 (Personick, 1984). Within the service sector, miscellaneous services will have the highest growth rate and provide the most new opportunities. This sector includes jobs in business services, such as management consulting, security, and data processing. Finance, insurance, real estate, and health and medical services are also expected to show

TABLE 8   Educational Attainment of the Civilian Labor Force, by Sex, Selected Years, 1959-1981

	Percentage Distribution						
	Elementary		High School		College		Median School
Year	Fewer than 5 years	5-8 years	1-3 years	4 years	1-3 years	4 years or more	Years Completed
	Males						
1959	6.1	26.9	20.2	27.2	9.1	10.4	11.5
1965	4.4	21.3	19.4	32.0	10.5	12.4	12.2
1970	2.9	16.9	17.5	35.1	13.5	14.2	12.4
1975	2.2	11.1	17.6	36.2	15.6	17.3	12.5
1980	1.5	8.3	16.0	36.5	17.7	20.0	12.7
1981	1.5	7.9	15.4	37.5	17.4	20.3	12.7
	Females						
1959	3.5	21.5	19.1	38.1	9.7	8.1	12.2
1965	2.4	16.6	18.7	41.9	10.4	10.0	12.3
1970	1.5	12.2	16.9	45.5	13.2	10.7	12.4
1975	1.0	8.1	17.6	44.7	15.4	13.3	12.5
1980	.7	5.5	14.9	45.0	18.1	15.9	12.6
1981	.8	5.1	14.2	45.5	18.6	15.7	12.7

SOURCE: Bureau of Labor Statistics (1982a:Table C-44).

above-average growth. Manufacturing industries, most hurt by the recent recession, are expected to rebound and to maintain a steady share of total employment of about 17 percent. Construction-related industries are also expected to rebound, growing slowly at 1 to 2 percent per annum through 1995. Electronic, computer, and other high-tech manufacturing industries are forecast to increase faster than total employment, but the total number of new jobs added to the economy by these industries is relatively small. Estimates of their contribution range from 3 to 17 percent of all new jobs through 1995 (Riche et al., 1983).

Growth, although slowed from previous years, is expected in wholesale and retail trade and in government. In the trade sector, eating and drinking establishments will provide a large number of new jobs. In government, a slowdown in job growth reflects budget reductions of the 1970s and declining school enrollments. As the children of the baby boom cohort enter their school years, an increase in the number of jobs in teaching is expected. The only industries for which job loss is projected are agriculture and private household services.

Occupational Outlook

Recent Trends

These broad industry directions, coupled with the introduction of new technologies, have resulted in several occupational trends, many of which gained momentum during the 1970s. In a study of "occupational winners and losers" over this decade, Leon (1982) found that winners—occupations that either added many jobs to the economy or that grew by 75 percent or more—were primarily in professional, managerial and administrative, technical, and clerical fields. Both criteria (large absolute numbers and high growth) were met by computer-related occupations, health technicians, and bank tellers. Job losses of 60,000 or more workers were posted primarily by blue-collar occupations. Big losses were seen among such occupations as delivery workers, operatives and assemblers in nondurable-consumer-goods-producing industries such as textiles, and in certain sectors of wholesale and retail trade, e.g., gas station attendants. As a result of these trends, by 1980 white-collar workers made up 50 percent of the work force. As Leon (1982:19) notes, women accounted for a disproportionate share of employment growth over the 1972–1980 period: 65 percent as compared with their 38 percent share of total employment in 1982. Many of the occupational winners were female-dominated occupations, and women accounted for virtually all the employment growth in such occupations as secretary, cashier, bookkeeper, bank teller, and welfare and health aide. In some cases (e.g., bookkeepers and teaching aides), this growth resulted in an increase in the already high proportion of women in these jobs.

Women also accounted for a large share of the increase in employment in male-intensive occupations. Thus, for example, women made up two-thirds of new accountants and 15 percent of new employment among engineers. They also made large relative gains among lawyers, computer specialists, and real estate agents and brokers. Even among slowly growing male-dominated jobs women made inroads. Thus, although only one in five new craft workers were women, their total representation rose from 3.6 percent in 1972 to 6 percent by 1980. Similarly, small but nonetheless real gains were made in other traditional male occupations, such as truck drivers and warehouse laborers.

Projections

The current distribution of employment across major occupational groups is compared to the projected distribution in Table 9. For the 1980s and 1990s BLS predicts that professional and technical employment will continue to

TABLE 9   Percentage Distribution of Employment,
by Major Occupational Group, 1982 and Projected to 1995

Occupational Group	1982	1995
Professional, technical and related workers	16	17
Managers, officials, and proprietors	9	10
Salesworkers	7	7
Clerical workers	19	19
Craft and related workers	11	12
Operatives	13	12
Service workers	16	16
Laborers, except farm	6	6
Farmers and farm workers	3	2

NOTE: Percentages may not add to 100 due to rounding.
SOURCE: Silvestri et al. (1984:Table 1).

increase at a rate greater than overall employment, fueled in part by the growth of high-tech industries. The rates of growth of managers, sales workers, and craft workers are expected to keep pace with overall growth. Operators and laborers will continue a long-term decline.

As a source of employment displacement and reconfiguration, the impact of new technologies on the job prospects of women (and men) is difficult to assess. Newer technologies appear to be moving with great speed and affecting a broad array of occupations (Serrin, 1983). Levitan and Johnson (1982) estimate that existing robotics technology could currently perform 7 million jobs, one-third of all manufacturing employment. Although any discussion of this subject is speculative at this point, clearly these technologies have implications for both "women's work" in the office and "men's work" on the shop floor. Already BLS projects that during the 1980s and 1990s office automation will begin to make significant inroads into clerical employment, with the result that these jobs will grow at slower rates than previously, although keeping pace with total job growth.

At the level of detailed occupations, Table 10 shows the 20 occupations that will grow most rapidly through 1995. Dominating the list are jobs in computers, newly emerging industries in data processing and business, and health services. Many of these jobs require a college degree or technical training. Three out of every four jobs for which data are available are dominated by either men or women. Table 11 shows the 20 top jobs in terms of growth in the number of new jobs. The list is led by more traditional occupations that have historically been large employers, for example, clerks, lower-level service workers, retail clerks, and truck drivers. Only a quarter of these jobs require a college degree (Silvestri et al., 1984:42), and four out of five are highly segregated by sex. The 20 jobs listed in Table 10

TABLE 10   The 20 Fastest-Growing Occupations, 1982–1995

Occupation	Percentage Growth[a]	Percentage Female[b]	Average Weekly Earnings[b]	Female:Male Earnings Ratio[b] (× 100)
1. Computer service technicians	96.8	NA	NA	NA
2. Legal assistants	94.3	NA	NA	NA
3. Computer systems analysts	85.3	25.1	$519	76.9
4. Computer programmers	76.9	28.4	422	73.6
5. Computer operators	75.8	63.2	260	67.8
6. Office machine repairers	71.7	5.6	327	—
7. Physical therapy assistants	67.8	82.7	209	—
8. Electrical engineers	65.3	3.5	549	—
9. Civil engineering technicians	63.9	17.8	348	75.3
10. Peripheral data-processing equipment operators	63.5	63.2	260	67.8
11. Insurance clerks, medical	62.2	NA	NA	NA
12. Electrical and electronic technicians	60.7	9.7	387	—
13. Occupational therapists	59.8	NA	NA	NA
14. Surveyor helpers	58.6	NA	NA	NA
15. Credit clerks, banking and insurance	54.1	NA	NA	NA
16. Physical therapists	53.6	67.3	305	67.3
17. Employment interviewers	52.5	48.7	402	64.3
18. Mechanical engineers	52.1	2.5	540	—
19. Mechanical engineering technicians	51.6	17.8	348	75.3
20. Compression and injection mold machine operators, plastics	50.3	NA	NA	NA
Total	25.0	39.5	$289	64.7

NOTES: NA = not available.

— = not shown because base is less than 50,000.

[a] Includes only detailed occupations with 1982 employment of 25,000 or more.

[b] Approximate due to use of different occupational classifications in sources. Data are based on 1981 annual averages; earnings refer to weekly earnings of full-time wage and salary workers in occupations of 50,000 or more.

SOURCES: Rytina (1982:Table 1) and Silvestri et al. (1984:Table 1).

are expected to add 1.6 million jobs to the economy by 1995; the jobs listed in Table 11 will add 9.2 million.

WOMEN'S STATUS IN THE LABOR MARKET
Trends in Job Segregation

As is apparent from the foregoing discussion, particular occupations are closely identified with and often performed almost exclusively by workers of one sex or the other. The distribution of women across major occupational

TABLE 11   The 20 Occupations With Largest Projected Job Growth Between 1982 and 1995

Occupation	Percentage Growth[a]	Percentage Female[b]	Average Weekly Earnings[b]	Female:Male Earnings Ratio[b] (× 100)
1. Building custodians	27.5	14.6	219	83.6
2. Cashiers	47.4	85.1	168	92.0
3. Secretaries	29.5	99.3	230	—
4. General clerks, office	29.6	83.5	192	—
5. Sales clerks	23.5	60.3	178	60.3
6. Nurses, registered	48.9	95.8	332	—
7. Waiters and waitresses	33.8	85.2	150	72.0
8. Teachers, kindergarten and elementary	37.4	82.2	322	82.2
9. Truck drivers	26.5	2.1	314	—
10. Nursing aides and orderlies	34.8	84.3	172	82.2
11. Sales representatives, technical	29.3	NA	NA	NA
12. Accountants and auditors	40.2	39.7	379	71.2
13. Automotive mechanics	38.3	.7	285	—
14. Supervisors of blue-collar workers	26.6	10.5	394	64.2
15. Kitchen helpers	35.9	30.5	135	—
16. Guards and doorkeepers	47.3	12.8	232	90.7
17. Food preparation and service workers, fast food restaurants	36.7	85.0	141	—
18. Managers, store	30.1	38.2	300	57.0
19. Carpenters	28.6	1.4	325	—
20. Electrical and electronic technicians	60.7	9.7	387	—
Total	25.0	39.5	$289	64.7

NOTES: NA = not available.
— = not shown because base is less than 50,000.
[a] Includes only detailed occupations with 1982 employment of 25,000 or more.
[b] Approximate due to use of different occupational classifications in sources. Data are based on 1981 annual averages; earnings refer to weekly earnings of full-time wage and salary workers in occupations of 50,000 or more.
SOURCES: Rytina (1982:Table 1) and Silvestri et al. (1984:Table 1).

categories is shown in Table 12 for 1970 and 1980. Although some changes have occurred (notably among executives and managers), certain categories remain highly sex-typed, e.g., clerical, other services, private household, craft workers, and laborers.

An overall index of the sex segregation of occupations has been developed that measures the minimum proportion or percentage of persons of either sex who would have to change to an occupation in which their sex is underrepresented in order for the occupational distributions of the sexes to be identical (Reskin and Hartmann, 1985). Segregation indices calculated since 1972

TABLE 12   Percentage Distribution of Women in Major Occupational
Groups, Change, and Rate of Growth in Female Representation, 1970–1980

Major Occupational Group	1970	1980	Change (1970–1980)	Rate of Growth
Executive, administrative, managerial	18.5	30.5	+12	.65
Professional specialty	44.3	49.1	+4.8	.11
Technicians	34.4	43.8	+1.8	.04
Sales	41.3	48.7	+7.4	.18
Administrative support, including clerical	73.2	77.1	+3.9	.05
Private household	96.3	95.3	−1.0	.01
Protective service	6.6	11.8	+5.2	.79
Other service	61.2	57.2	−4.0	.07
Farming, forestry, fishing	9.1	14.9	+5.8	.64
Precision production, including craft	7.3	7.8	+0.5	.07
Machine operators	39.7	40.7	+1.0	.03
Transportation	4.2	7.8	+3.6	.86
Handlers, laborers	17.5	19.8	+2.3	.13

NOTE: Both 1970 and 1980 data are coded to the 1980 census occupational classification.
SOURCE: Rytina and Bianchi (1984:Table 2).

across detailed occupations show a decline from 68.3 to 61.7 (Reskin and
Hartmann, 1985). Beller and Han (1984) developed several sets of segregation projections, all of which extrapolate 1970 trends to the 1980s. By most
of their estimates, the segregation index will continue to drop, to about 60.0
by 1990. Their most optimistic forecast, however, shows a drop to 41.3. The
magnitude of these declines can be better understood by comparing them
with the decline of 25 percentage points that Blau and Hendricks (1979)
estimated would occur if past hiring remained in place but new hiring was
fully integrated or blind with regard to sex.

The value of the segregation index is affected by two factors: the number
of people employed in different sex-typed occupations (the mix effect) and
the sex composition of workers within an occupation (the composition
effect). Blau and Hendricks (1979) found an increase in segregation during
the 1950s, which was primarily due to the considerable growth of female-
dominated occupations, notably clerical workers and professions such as
teaching and social work. During the 1960s the segregation index declined
as the growth of female-dominated jobs slowed and the share of workers
(predominantly men) entering jobs held largely by the opposite sex
increased. Using Current Population Survey data, Beller (1982) found that
these trends continued during the 1970s and accounted for much of the
decline in segregation in this period. A recent study by Rytina and Bianchi
(1984) examined changes in the sex composition of occupations using

results of the 1970 and 1980 censuses. Their findings corroborate and expand those of Beller and Han (1984). They too found a decline in segregation during the 1970s, which resulted from three factors: (1) a substantial drop in male-intensive occupations—those in which 20 percent or less of workers were women; (2) a modest rise in sex-neutral occupations—those employing 21 to 59 percent women; and (3) no increase in the number of female-dominated occupations—those with 60 percent or more female incumbents. Thus, in terms of employment, both men and women were more likely to be in neutral or integrated occupations by 1980. Neither men nor women, however, were significantly more likely to be in occupations dominated by the opposite sex, so that the occupations that were most closely identified with one sex or the other remained that way over the decade.

Thus, there was little or no change in the sex composition of jobs in major female-intensive categories such as clerical and private household workers, nor in male-intensive categories such as transportation, laborer, or craft worker. The single greatest change occurred among managers, a category in which women increased from 18 to 31 percent of total employment. For both men and women, movement into sex-neutral occupations coincided with declines in employment in traditionally sex-dominated jobs.

Several features of this apparent decrease in job segregation are worth noting. First, change appears to be greatest in occupations at the upper end of the socioeconomic spectrum—among managers, professionals, and technicians—occupations that employ a relatively small proportion of the total labor force, either male or female. Second, as Rytina and Bianchi (1984) point out, within sex-neutral or integrated occupations, segregation is still possible within subspecialties or in jobs within firms. For example, in a study of several hundred establishments, Bielby and Baron (1984) found that job classifications were almost completely segregated. They also found that the level of segregation remained constant over the 20-year period from 1959 to 1979, during which equal employment opportunity laws were passed and visibly enforced. In summary, although there have been changes in the sex composition of individual occupations, recent trends and projections for the future reveal only modest change in and persistent high levels of job segregation.

On a more optimistic note, there are a number of considerations that would lead one to predict a continued decrease in job segregation. It appears that younger women, who are new or recent entrants to the labor force, are taking the lead in moving into nontraditional occupations (Beller, 1982; Reskin and Hartmann, 1985). As may already be occurring, the relative shortfall of young male workers, coupled with the rising work aspirations of young women, could enhance employers' receptivity to hiring women for nontra-

ditional jobs. Employers may also be less likely to rely on outmoded stereotypes to screen and place women in segregated jobs. The higher pay, on
average, of nontraditional or male-dominated jobs may also make them
increasingly attractive to women who maintain families or who contribute a
large share of household income in dual-worker couples. Women's acquisi-
tion of more work experience, education, and training should result as well
in greater job market savvy, enabling them to better identify and take advantage of favorable job opportunities.

The highly visible progress of women in professional occupations also
enhances the position of women by providing role models and a sense of
empowerment, thereby initiating an effect that would ultimately benefit
women at all levels of the occupational structure.

The projected slowdown in male-dominated manufacturing jobs and in
female-dominated clerical jobs could also be conducive to greater integration if future trends follow the patterns of the 1970s. During that decade,
decline in traditional, segregated occupations coincided with movement into
integrated or sex-neutral ones rather than leading to the creation of new
male- or female-dominated bastions.

Projected changes in the age and race or ethnic composition of the future
labor force also have potential implications for job segregation. Although
there is considerable controversy over the effectiveness of existing affirmative action programs, which set goals and timetables for the recruitment and
hiring of protected classes of workers, the existence of these programs
serves, at a minimum, to legitimate the right of women to enter nontraditional occupations. These programs typically target workers for entry-level
jobs and accordingly have been aimed at younger workers. The declining
numbers of younger workers might change their focus in favor of older,
returning workers, among whom women would figure prominently. But the
changing demography of the labor force could also lead to stagnation or
erosion of women's position in the labor market. As the number of younger,
minority workers increases through immigration and as a result of race
differentials in fertility, women's concerns (which are neither mutually
exclusive nor identical with those of minorities) may lose visibility. A similar competition may also arise between the interests of women and minority
workers and those of older white male workers. Age discrimination legislation passed in 1967 sets the stage for an increasing number of lawsuits
pertaining to layoffs and early retirements. If these cases are successful,
worker turnover will be slowed and white men stand to benefit at the expense
of wider opportunities for younger or less experienced workers.

The projected high rates of growth of many female-dominated occupations might also tend to slow the decline in job segregation, since women
could be expected to seek out or be recruited for occupations in which they

had already established entry. This tendency might be especially pronounced among mothers of young children and reentering women (who will account for most of the upcoming increase in female labor force participation), because they are less knowledgeable about the job market and potentially more constrained in their choices by virtue of family responsibilities. This possible trend might be offset, however, by a movement of female heads of household into higher-paying, male-dominated jobs.

Another factor that would tend to maintain segregation at current levels is the increasingly smaller size of cohorts entering the labor force. Because of their smaller numbers, younger cohorts would have to enter nontraditional occupations at extremely high rates in order to prompt significant changes in the sex composition of given occupations. Younger women are pacesetters; however, the majority of them still aspire to and enter female-dominated jobs (Marini and Brinton, 1984). Contributing to this more pessimistic prognosis is the fact that much of the decline in job segregation to date has reflected the activities of an extremely large cohort in the early stages of their work lives. This is a period of especially great experimentation and job mobility. Since job and occupation switching decline with age (Rytina, 1983), the rate of movement into and out of occupations could slow as the baby boom cohort settles down to particular jobs or careers, thus slowing changes in the sex composition of jobs.

In view of these tendencies pointing in opposite directions, it is difficult to predict future changes in the degree of job segregation. On balance, demographic factors suggest a slowing in the rate of decrease in segregation that was observed in the 1970s. Yet a strong women's movement or government enforcement effort coupled with economic growth could certainly contribute to further substantial decline.

The Wage Gap

The persistence of a considerable disparity in the pay of full-time, year-round male and female workers has been labeled the "wage gap." Typically the wage gap is measured as the ratio of female-to-male median annual or hourly earnings, or in terms of the actual dollar difference between them. Since 1955, women's earnings relative to those of men have fluctuated at around 60 percent (U.S. Department of Labor, 1982:Table 12). In 1982 the ratio had moved to 62.0 percent, which represented a difference in annual earnings of $7,976 (Norwood, 1984). In constant dollars, from 1955 to 1981, the earnings gap increased by 60 percent, from $1,911 in 1955 to $3,032 in 1981 (U.S. Department of Labor, 1982). As Norwood (1984) notes, the size of the wage gap shrinks as additional considerations such as occupation, education, work experience, and age are taken into account.

Thus, for example, looking at 1981 salary levels for a group of narrowly defined white-collar jobs, Sieling (1984) found that the earnings gap was in the 0 to 16 percent range, smallest within the same establishments, and not always in men's favor.

O'Neill (1983) argues that trends in the wage gap can be explained in part by the changing composition of the female labor force and concomitant changes in women's standing relative to men on productivity-related characteristics. Thus, with the influx of women into the labor force in the 1960s and 1970s, the level of education of employed women as well as their work experience declined and the wage gap widened. The narrowing of these differentials did not appear to influence the wage gap until about 1979; since that time there has been a slight improvement in women's favor. O'Neill notes that the decline in the gap was greatest for workers ages 25 to 34. She concludes that wage differentials are likely to narrow in the next decade as young women work more continuously, increase their education, and raise their work expectations.

Another study, which projected men's and women's pay to the year 2000, concurred with this assessment (Smith and Ward, 1984). By estimating the earnings of future female labor force participants and averaging them with those of women already in the labor force, they arrived at a projected average wage for all women. Their findings indicate that if current labor force trends were to continue, women would earn 74 percent of what men do by the end of the century—narrowing but not closing the wage gap from approximately 40 to 25 percent.

In contrast to these optimistic assessments, a recent study by Green (1983) found that the wage gap widened from 1970 to 1980 for recent labor force entrants, despite the fact that the productivity-related characteristics of males and females became more similar over this period. Green also followed the progress of the cohort of workers who entered the labor force in 1970 by examining outcomes for a panel of experienced workers in 1980. Among whites he found that the male-female wage gap widened from 14 to 32 percent. Thus, after 10 years of potential work experience, the wage gap of the experienced 1970 cohort approximated the overall gap of about 38 percent for the entire labor force.

Because there was no direct measure of work experience in Green's data, some amount of the observed gap could be due to unmeasured breaks in women's actual work experience, particularly that of married women. Yet the trends in women's labor force participation reviewed earlier suggest that this cohort had relatively high levels of activity.

Green's results suggest instead that there had been a substantial increase in sex discrimination, especially against white women, over the last decade. By his estimates, discrimination (including discrimination in wages and occupational placement) could have accounted for as much as 79 percent of the gap in 1980, compared with 43 percent in 1970. Green's results also indicate that occupational segregation was more important in explaining wage differences for entry-level workers, while wage discrimination was more important among experienced workers. He speculated that the lack of progress by white women (compared with that of black men, who did make wage gains relative to white men) may be due to heightened job competition among women and minority men and to the role of equal employment and affirmative action programs in awarding jobs.

Studies of male-female earnings differences that have been conducted over the last 15 years also conclude that some portion (as much as 30 to 40 percent) of the wage gap is due to discrimination (see Treiman and Hartmann, 1981, for a review). Although there is considerable controversy surrounding the use of residual or unexplained variation to estimate its impact (see, for example, Cole 1979), to the extent that discrimination exists (and may be increasing), it augurs badly for women's achievement of equal pay.

Because the more women there are in an occupation the less it pays (Treiman and Hartmann, 1981), job segregation is a significant factor in maintaining wage differentials. Thus, the mixed prospects for a decline in segregation do not bode well for women's progress in closing the wage gap. Moreover, occupational projections indicate that a large number of new jobs will be in what have been historically low-paying sectors, e.g., retail sales, maintenance work, and lower-level health care jobs. Thus, the weekly earnings of about half the large-growth jobs in Table 11 fall below the labor-force-wide average. A recent study (Bluestone et al., 1984) concludes that by the year 2000 most jobs will be in sectors of the economy that currently have average annual earnings of less than $12,500 and there will be a substantial decline in jobs in industries paying more than $22,000 per year. Unless women are able to move in significant numbers out of the jobs in which they are now concentrated, they are likely to be found disproportionately in these low-paying sectors. At the same time, women's inroads in professional occupations do signal substantially improved earnings prospects for a relatively small, elite group. In addition, for women workers in other occupational groups, increased unionization may improve earnings (Freeman and Leonard, 1984).

A large portion of the pay gap (another 30 to 40 percent) is due to differences in the productivity-related characteristics of men and women in the same occupations. The prospects for narrowing these male-female differentials appear better, as the studies cited earlier by O'Neill (1983) and Smith and Ward (1984) indicate. Women's accrual of more on-the-job training, tenure within a firm, and seniority should result in higher earnings, assuming that men and women receive similar rates of return on these factors. To the extent that women's rates of return are lower than those of men (Roos, 1981), however, the wage gap will not close, at least not as much as predicted.

Even under the most optimistic assumptions, it appears that a sizable wage gap will persist through the end of the century. Wage gap comparisons, however, typically take into account only full-time, year-round workers. Because part-time work is expected to increase throughout the economy and because women's rate of part-time work is likely to remain much higher than that of men, the real wage gap between men and women is indeed much larger than the foregoing estimates suggest. Although part-time work appears to be attractive to women who are juggling family responsibilities, it appears to offer little or no wage growth (Corcoran et al., 1984). More insidiously, women's higher rates of involuntary part-time work and their increasing propensity to hold multiple jobs suggest that women are being channeled into, rather than choosing, this option.

The increased presence of women in the labor force has led to several developments that, if successful, could hasten a closing of the wage gap. Foremost among these is the push for comparable worth or pay equity. Comparable worth strategies seek to raise the wages of traditional female-dominated jobs. Comparable worth advocates argue that pay should reflect the skill, effort, and responsibility entailed in jobs and that jobs with similar features should be paid the same whether they are performed by women or men. Comparable worth has made considerable, rapid progress, especially in the public sector. It has been implemented by several state and local governments and is increasingly the basis of collective bargaining and organizing efforts. Numerous studies, preliminary to establishment of a pay equity policy, are also under way (Dean et al., 1984). Moreover, several recent court decisions have encouraged comparable worth claims. The Supreme Court's 1981 ruling in *Gunther* v. *County of Washington, Oregon* (101 S. Ct. 2242) opened the door to such claims, because it found that claims of wage discrimination in *different* jobs could be heard under Title VII; the Court specifically denied, however, that it was endorsing comparable worth. A 1983 U.S. district court ruling against Washington State (which is still under appeal) upheld the validity of a comparable worth strategy and particularly the use of a job evaluation plan by the state to determine comparable jobs. Thus far, successful comparable worth strategies have succeeded in raising wages among female-dominated jobs in the clerical, health, social work, and nursing fields.

When earnings growth for men is examined by age or over the life cycle, it is found to be greatest during the late 20s and 30s, a period that coincides with the years of women's peak childbearing and rearing. To the extent that women's labor force attachment during this time can be enhanced, the payoff in increased earnings should be especially pronounced. Thus, other developments, such as the increased interest in child care and alternative work arrangements, also have potentially favorable implications for women's pay. Access to more and better child care and the availability of schedules that are conducive to meeting family demands should increase women's ability to go to work and stay on the job.

The strength of these developments in the face of a political environment in which equal employment goals have been neglected attests to the urgency of the needs of women workers. Their own activism and organizing efforts on these fronts are perhaps the greatest basis for optimism that the wage gap will continue to narrow.

IMPLICATIONS FOR FUTURE RESEARCH

In light of the foregoing discussion, a research agenda to better illuminate these issues might include the following topics:

1. Sophisticated modeling and simulation exercises to better assess future directions in sex segregation and pay equity in light of demographic and economic changes. Such efforts need to explicitly incorporate (a) the age structure both of the labor force and of occupations; (b) age differences in job and occupational mobility; (c) cohort size and race and ethnic composition; (d) effects of changes in sex composition on occupational wages; and (e) training and skill needs (the last two factors were not dealt with in this paper but need to be taken into account in any large-scale modeling effort).

2. Inquiry into the overall and possibly disparate impact of technological change on men and women's occupational distribution and pay.

3. Better understanding of the nature of work in newly emerging industries, with a special focus on unionizing efforts and on those seeking to introduce innovative forms of workplace organization.

4. Examination of the economic interests of and prospects for coalition or competition between women and minorities (male and female, foreign- and native-born).

5. An inquiry into the impact of child care and alternative work arrangements on labor force attachment and job choice, because most of the projected increase in women's labor force participation will come from the mothers of young children.

6. Case studies to investigate the so-called sex-neutral occupations (which account for much of the recent decline in sex segregation) to better understand some of the factors that appear to promote the entry of both men and women.

7. Now that comparable worth is beginning to be implemented, albeit still on a limited basis, evaluation of its scope and impact in increasing the wages of particular "women's" jobs and of its implications for levels of employment in affected jobs and for the sex composition of workers in them.

REFERENCES

Andreassen, A.J., N.C. Saunders, and B.W. Wu
  1984　Economic outlook for the 1990's, three scenarios for economic growth. Pp. 9–21 in Bureau of Labor Statistics, *Employment Projections for 1995*. Washington, D.C.: U.S. Department of Labor.

Beller, A.
  1982　Occupational segregation by sex: Determinants and changes. *Journal of Human Resources* 17(3):371–372.

Beller, A., and K. Han
  1984　Occupational sex segregation: Prospects for the 1980s. Pp. 91–114 in B. Reskin, ed., *Sex Segregation in the Workplace: Trends, Explanations, Remedies*. Committee on Women's Employment and Related Social Issues. Washington, D.C.: National Academy Press.

Bielby, W., and J. Baron
  1984　A women's place is with other women: Sex segregation within organizations. Pp. 27–55 in B. Reskin, ed., *Sex Segregation in the Workplace: Trends, Explanations, Remedies*. Committee on Women's Employment and Related Social Issues. Washington, D.C.: National Academy Press.

Blau, F.D., and W.E. Hendricks
  1979　Occupational segregation by sex: Trends and prospects. *Journal of Human Resources* 14(2):197–210.

Blau, F.D., and L.M. Kahn
  1981　Race and sex differences in quits by young workers. *Industrial and Labor Relations Review* 34(4):563–577.

Bluestone, B., B. Harrison, and L. Gorham
  1984　Storm Clouds on the Horizon: Labor Market Crisis and Industrial Policy. Economic Education Project, Brookline, Mass.

Bureau of Labor Statistics
  1982a　*Labor Force Statistics Derived From the Current Population Survey: Databook*. Vol. 1. Washington, D.C.: U.S. Department of Labor.
  1982b　*BLS Handbook of Methods*. Washington, D.C.: U.S. Department of Labor.
  1983a　*Women at Work: A Chartbook*. Washington, D.C.: U.S. Department of Labor.
  1983b　*Marital and Family Patterns of Workers: An Update*. Washington, D.C.: U.S. Department of Labor.
  1984a　*Employment Projections for 1995*. Washington, D.C.: U.S. Department of Labor.
  1984b　*Families at Work: The Jobs and the Pay*. Washington, D.C.: U.S. Department of Labor.

Chiswick, B.R.
  1982　Immigrants in the U.S. labor market. *Annals of the American Academy of Political and Social Science* 460(1):64–72.

Cole, J.
  1979　*Fair Science: Women in the Scientific Community*. New York: Columbia University Press.

Corcoran, M., G. Duncan, and M. Ponza
  1984   Work experience, job segregation, and wages. Pp. 171-191 in B. Reskin, ed., *Sex Segregation in the Workplace: Trends, Explanations, Remedies*. Committee on Women's Employment and Related Social Issues. Washington, D.C.: National Academy Press.
Dean, V., J.A. Grune, M. Klaw, and D. Mitchell
  1984   Who's Working for Working Women? National Committee on Pay Equity, Washington, D.C..
Finch, J.L.
  1983   Worklife estimates should be consistent with labor force rates. *Monthly Labor Review* 106(6):34-36.
Freeman, R.B., and J.S. Leonard
  1984   Union Maids: Unions and the Female Workforce. Unpublished paper, Conference on Gender in the Workplace, Brookings Institution, Washington, D.C.
Fullerton, H.N., and J. Tschetter
  1984   The 1995 labor force: A second look. Pp. 1-8 in Bureau of Labor Statistics, *Employment Projections for 1995*. Washington, D.C.: U.S. Department of Labor.
Green, G.W.
  1983   Wage Differentials for Job Entrants, by Race and Sex. Unpublished Ph.D. dissertation, Department of Economics, George Washington University.
Haber, S.E., E.J. Lamas, and G. Green
  1983   A new method for estimating job separation rates by sex and age. *Monthly Labor Review* 106(6):20-27.
Johnson, B.L., and E. Waldman
  1984   Most women who maintain families receive poor labor market returns. Pp. 15-19 in Bureau of Labor Statistics, *Families at Work: The Jobs and the Pay*. Washington, D.C.: U.S. Department of Labor.
Keely, C.B.
  1979   *U.S. Immigration: A Policy Analysis*. New York: Population Council.
Leon, C.B.
  1982   Occupation winners and losers: Who they were during 1972-80. *Monthly Labor Review* 105(6):18-28.
Levitan, S.A., and C.M. Johnson
  1982   The future of work: Does it belong to us or the robots? *Monthly Labor Review* 105(9):10-14.
Lloyd, C.B., and B.T. Niemi
  1979   *The Economics of Sex Differentials*. New York: Columbia University Press.
Marini, M.M., and M.C. Brinton
  1984   Sex typing in occupational socialization. Pp. 192-232 in B. Reskin, ed., *Sex Segregation in the Workplace: Trends, Explanations, Remedies*. Committee on Women's Employment and Related Social Issues. Washington, D.C.: National Academy Press.
Mellor, E.F.
  1984   Investigating differences in weekly earnings of women and men. *Monthly Labor Review* 107(6):17-28.
Norwood, J.
  1984   Working Women and Public Policy. Address presented at the National Conference on Women, the Economy and Public Policy, Washington, D.C.
O'Neill, J.A.
  1983   The Trend in the Sex Differential in Wages. Working paper, Urban Institute, Washington, D.C.

Personick, V.A.
  1984   The job outlook through 1995: Industry output and employment projections. Pp. 22–34
          in Bureau of Labor Statistics, *Employment Projections for 1995*. Washington, D.C.:
          U.S. Department of Labor.
Reskin, B.F., and H.I. Hartmann, eds.
  1985   *Women's Work, Men's Work: Sex Segregation on the Job*. Committee on Women's
          Employment and Related Social Issues. Washington, D.C.: National Academy Press.
Riche, R.W., D.E. Hecker, and J.O. Burgan
  1983   High technology today and tomorrow: A small slice of the employment pie. *Monthly
          Labor Review* 106(11):50–58.
Roos, P.A.
  1981   Sex stratification in the workplace: Male-female differences in returns to occupation.
          Social Science Research 10(3):195–224.
Rytina, N.F.
  1982   Earnings of men and women: A look at specific occupations. *Monthly Labor Review*
          105(4):25–31.
  1983   Occupational changes and tenure, 1981. Pp. 4-34 in Bureau of Labor Statistics, *Job
          Tenure and Occupational Change, 1981*. Washington, D.C.: U.S. Department of
          Labor.
Rytina, N.F., and S.M. Bianchi
  1984   Occupational reclassification and changes in distribution by gender. *Monthly Labor
          Review* 107(3):11–17.
Sekscenski, E.S.
  1981   Women's share of moonlighting nearly doubles during 1969–79. Pp. 36–39 in Bureau of
          Labor Statistics, *Multiple Jobholders in May 1979*. Washington, D.C.: U.S. Depart-
          ment of Labor.
Serrin, W.
  1983   "High tech" is no job panacea, experts say. *New York Times* (Nov. 18).
  1984   Shifts in work put white men in the minority. *New York Times* (July 31).
Sieling, M.S.
  1984   Staffing patterns prominent in female-male earnings gap. *Monthly Labor Review* (6):29–
          33.
Silvestri, G.T., J.M. Lukasiewicz, and M.E. Einstein
  1984   Occupational employment projections through 1995. Pp. 35–47 in Bureau of Labor
          Statistics, *Employment Projections for 1995*. Washington, D.C.: U.S. Department of
          Labor.
Smith, J.P., and M. Ward
  1984   *Women's Wages and Work in the Twentieth Century*. Santa Monica, Calif.: Rand Corpo-
          ration.
Smith, R.E., ed.
  1979   *The Subtle Revolution*. Washington, D.C.: Urban Institute.
Smith, S.J.
  1982   New worklife estimates reflect changing profile of labor force. *Monthly Labor Review*
          105(3):15–20.
  1983   Labor force participation rates are not the relevant factor. *Monthly Labor Review*
          106(6):36–38.
Treiman, D.J., and H.I. Hartmann, eds.
  1981   *Women, Work, and Wages: Equal Pay for Jobs of Equal Value*. Committee on Occupa-
          tional Classification and Analysis. Washington, D.C.: National Academy Press.

U.S. Department of Labor
   1982   *Equal Employment Opportunities for Women: U.S. Policies*. Washington, D.C.: U.S.
           Department of Labor.
Viscusi, W.K.
   1980   Sex differences in worker quitting. *Review of Economics and Statistics* 62(3):388–398.
Waite, L.J.
   1978   Projecting female labor force participation from sex-role attitudes. *Social Science
           Research* 7(4):299–318.
Waldman, E.
   1984   Labor force statistics from a family perspective. Pp. 1–5 in Bureau of Labor Statistics,
           Families at Work: The Jobs and the Pay. Washington, D.C.: U.S. Department of Labor.

Biographical Sketches of Authors

BARBARA R. BERGMANN is professor of economics at the University of Maryland. Her special interests include sex roles in the economy and the computer simulation of economic systems. She previously taught at Brandeis University and has served as senior economist at the Council of Economic Advisers, the Agency for International Development, and The Brookings Institution. She has written on feminist economics, the theory of discrimination, the economic support of children, and income inequality, and has testified often in employment discrimination and comparable worth cases and in congressional hearings. She has written on current economic affairs for the *New York Times* and the *Los Angeles Times*. She has a Ph.D. degree in economics from Harvard University.

PAMELA STONE CAIN is associate professor of sociology at Hunter College, City University of New York. She teaches, conducts research, writes, and lectures on topics related to women in the labor force, among them, job segregation, comparable worth, and job evaluation. She previously served as special assistant to the president of the college and was a member of the staff of the Committee on Occupational Classification and Analysis at the National Research Council. She has a B.A. from Duke University and a Ph.D. from Johns Hopkins University, both in sociology.

HEIDI I. HARTMANN is study director of both the Committee on Women's Employment and Related Social Issues and the Panel on Technology and Women's Employment at the National Research Council. She previously

168 BIOGRAPHICAL SKETCHES

served as associate executive director of the Commission on Behavioral and Social Sciences and Education and as research associate to the Committee on Occupational Classification and Analysis. In that capacity she coedited (with Donald J. Treiman) the committee's final report on comparable worth. Her research has concentrated on employment issues related to women and minorities, particularly discrimination and internal labor markets, and on political economy and feminist theory. She is the author of several articles on women's economic status; she lectures frequently on that and other topics and has testified in congressional hearings on comparable worth. She has a B.A. from Swarthmore College and M.Ph. and Ph.D. degrees from Yale University, all in economics.

MARK R. KILLINGSWORTH is associate professor of economics at Rutgers University and research economist at the National Bureau of Economic Research. His research interests include employment discrimination, labor supply, and immigration. He has served as a consultant to parties involved in litigation under Title VII of the Civil Rights Act, including the Equal Employment Opportunity Commission, the Department of Labor, and the Department of Justice and has presented testimony on comparable worth to the Joint Economic Committee of the U.S. Congress. He has a B.A. from the University of Michigan and M.Ph. and D.Ph. degrees from the University of Oxford, where he was a Rhodes scholar.

LESLIE ZEBROWITZ MCARTHUR is professor of psychology at Brandeis University. Her principal research interests are in the area of social perception and have included people's causal explanations for their own and others' behavior, cognitive bases of stereotyping, and the nonverbal communication of personality impressions. She has a B.A. degree from the University of Wisconsin and M.S. and Ph.D. degrees from Yale University, all in psychology.

PATRICIA A. ROOS is assistant professor of sociology at the State University of New York at Stony Brook. She was a staff member of the National Research Council's Committee on Occupational Classification and Analysis. She has conducted research on institutional factors contributing to sex segregation in the workplace, cross-cultural research on sex differences in occupational attainment, and analyses of ethnic differences in occupational and earnings attainment. She has a B.A. from the University of California, Davis, and a Ph.D. from the University of California at Los Angeles, both in sociology.

JAMES E. ROSENBAUM is associate professor of sociology and education at Northwestern University. Previously he was associate professor of sociology at Yale University. His work focuses on institutional mechanisms within organizations that affect employees' career attainments and compensation. He has just completed a book on the topic, and he is now extending this work in a project funded by the Russell Sage Foundation. He received a B.A. from Yale University and M.A. and Ph.D. degrees from the Department of Social Relations at Harvard University.

DONALD P. SCHWAB is Donald C. Slichter Research Professor at the University of Wisconsin. His Ph.D. is from the University of Minnesota where he majored in industrial relations. He teaches and conducts research on personnel/human resources and organizational behavior. He is a fellow of the Academy of Management and the American Psychological Association, and he is a member of the editorial boards of the *Academy of Management Journal* and *Organizational Behavior and Human Performance*. He has been a visiting faculty member at the universities of Minnesota and Kentucky.

DONALD J. TREIMAN is professor of sociology at the University of California at Los Angeles. His research interests center on the comparative study of social stratification and social mobility. He has written extensively on problems of occupational classification and measurement, including a book analyzing occupational prestige data from 60 countries. Previously he served as study director of the Committee on Occupational Classification and Analysis at the National Research Council, which produced reports on job evaluation, comparable worth, and the *Dictionary of Occupational Titles*; he was also study director of the Committee on Basic Research in the Behavioral and Social Sciences, which produced two volumes on the value and usefulness of basic research. He has a B.A. from Reed College, and M.A. and Ph.D. degrees from the University of Chicago, all in sociology.

Index